School Library
Media Programs:
Focus on

No. 10

W9-CPG-802

At the Pirate Academy

Adventures with Language in the Library Media Center

GARY ZINGHER

American Library Association / Chicago and London 1990

School Media Centers: Focus on Trends and Issues

CULTURAL PLURALISM AND CHILDREN'S MEDIA by Ester Dyer

PROJECTING A POSITIVE IMAGE THROUGH PUBLIC RELATIONS by Cosette Kies

THE TEACHING ROLE OF THE SCHOOL MEDIA SPECIALIST by Kay E. Vandergrift

A PLACE FOR CARING AND CELEBRATION by Ralph Peterson

A STUDY OF COMBINED SCHOOL-PUBLIC LIBRARIES by Shirley Aaron

INSTRUCTIONAL DESIGN AND THE LIBRARY MEDIA SPECIALIST by Margaret E. Chisholm and Donald P. Ely

MANAGING THE BUILDING-LEVEL SCHOOL LIBRARY MEDIA PROGRAM by Warren B. Hicks

INVOLVING THE SCHOOL LIBRARY MEDIA SPECIALIST IN CURRICULUM DEVELOPMENT by Betty P. Cleaver and William D. Taylor

continued by

School Library Media Programs: Focus on Trends and Issues, edited by Eleanor Kulleseid

THE INSTRUCTIONAL CONSULTANT ROLE OF THE SCHOOL LIBRARY MEDIA SPECIALIST by Betty P. Cleaver and William D. Taylor

AT THE PIRATE ACADEMY by Gary Zingher

Library of Congress Cataloging-in-Publication Data

Zingher, Gary.
    At the pirate academy : adventures with language in the library media center / by Gary Zingher.
        p. cm. — (School library media programs. Focus on trends and issues)
    Includes bibliographical references.
    ISBN 0-8389-3384-X
    1. School libraries—Activity programs.   2. Media programs (Education)   I. Title.   II. Series.
    Z675.S3Z48   1990   90-1074
    027.8'223--dc20

Printed in the United States of America.

94 93 92 91 90   5 4 3 2 1

Contents

Acknowledgments

To my fellow journeymen and teachers: Rodney Lathan, Moses Gardner, Joe Kaso, and the Kuemmerleins.

To my editor, Betty Kulleseid, for investing her soul in this project and enriching it with her deep sense of the ways children learn.

To Linda Greengrass, my colleague in developing and teaching the *Creative Library Programs* course at Bank Street College, for all her knowledge and support the last two years in both matters of technology and literature. To Susan Hirsch, who showed me the paths to Bank Street and Manhattan Country School.

To my brother Rick for his developmental understanding, my sister Cindy for the many nourishing weekends, and my Pennsylvania family: Donna, Sandy, and Adam, for their encouragement and humor.

To the children of Manhattan Country School, who so often joined me in magical alliances.

To our director, Gus Trowbridge, whose extraordinary vision of a school embraced the idea of the library as a place for the imagination.

To Kallyn Krash and Lois Gelernt, the godmothers of the library program, who brought enthusiasm, insight, and guidance every step of the journey.

To my friend Michèle Solá, who helped me articulate my vision and think about the shape and content of this book.

To my bright and adventurous partners: Cynthia Rogers, Jean Finnerty, and Doris Finkel, who made possible so many worlds and celebrations including the Comedy Museum, the Caravan, and Marketplace, and the Mythic Tribal Plays.

To Jane Dickson, David Iasevoli, Ann Kaplan, Tim Arnold, and Emily Dreifus for their friendship, faith, and good spirits both in and out of school.

To Susan Harris for her sensitive contributions to the Night Festival. To Dianne Cherr-Bachman for inspiring the Caravan Mural and the Entrances to

Fantasy Lands. To Junius Harris and Toni Savage, who sparked the County Fair and other events with their energy and playfulness. To Christine Poff, who helped me to focus on issues of equality and social justice. To Marty Trowbridge for her invaluable work behind the scenes. To Gloria Brown for always being there as our school hearth and anchor.

And to Jan Campbell, Martha Foote, Anne Schiller, Laura Daigen, Rachel Walpole, David McKnight, Mary Trowbridge, Patty Trimble, Emily Edwards, Carol O'Donnell, Jon Zeitlin, Kelvina Butcher, Leena Reddy, Helen Russell, Chris Iijima, Marino Regino, Leo Reynoso, Mei Mei Sanford, Anne Zinnser, Sandy Jordan, Chona Colayco, Lisa Petterson, Rosie Elliott, Susan Brudos, Vicki Camp, Edward Jewett, Ed Fersch, Ginny Scheer, Oak Sinatra, Emily Ryan Lerner, Ruth Gieschen, Sister Margaret Dennehy, Gary Tannenbaum, Jocelyn Chait, Richard Sung, Roberta Altman, and my scrabble buddies: Clint Ingram and David Levinson Wilk.

Introduction

School library media specialists are, by and large, reflective practitioners. They reflect on their own work with students, and on the efforts of other educators in their schools. This book is the tangible outcome of one intuitive and successful practitioner's seven-year journey. Gary Zingher works in an unusual setting. The Manhattan Country School, founded in 1966 by its current director, Augustus Trowbridge, is a multicultural, ethnically integrated independent school whose progressive philosophy is best expressed in the school's overview:

> Our goal is for students to be open-minded and compassionate, to gain a sense of themselves and others, and to understand and appreciate the diversity of the human condition. We want our students to be well trained in the basic academic disciplines, to fulfill their creative potential, and to gain satisfaction in their physical, emotional, and social development. We want students to love learning, and to value knowledge, creativity, and humor. Finally, we hope they will be responsible, critical and caring members of a pluralistic society who recognize that they have the power and resources to effect change and who have the self-esteem and confidence to pursue their dreams.

The school is housed in a six-story landmark building near Central Park, Spanish Harlem, Mount Sinai Hospital, the Cooper-Hewett Museum, and the Jewish Museum. Although small in number, the student population is as diverse as the neighborhood, and represents many ethnic and socioeconomic backgrounds. There are ten classes (pre-kindergarten through eighth grade) and an enrollment of 185 children. The six youngest classes are organized into mixed age groupings; readers will, therefore, find classes often identified by age rather than grade. For example, the fours/fives are a mixed Pre-K–Kindergarten group; fives/sixes are a Kindergarten-Grade One group, and so on up to the nines/tens, or Fourth-Fifth Grade group.

The author, a former play therapist and creative dramatics specialist, has brought to this setting an approach to teaching and literature that is compatible with the school's values. He has been able to pursue a highly individual vision of library programming, one on which other practitioners may draw to inspire changes in their own programs, regardless of setting.

Most library media professionals perform a balancing act with two instructional modes. One is the teacher-directed information skills mode that relies more on cognitive, left-brain, rational problem solving. The library media specialist functions as an information expert, often using technology to organize and provide access to an expanding universe of knowledge in many formats.

The other mode is the student-oriented literature appreciation or reader's advisory mode, characterized more by affective, interactional, right-brain, intuitive problem solving. The library media specialist functions as a pied piper, luring the young into book worlds as a reader and weaver of story, a celebrator of sound and image.

Both modes are vital to students of all ages, and both lead to learning and development of critical thinking. Yet most library media specialists tend to move on a continuum from the playful and aesthetic pied piper mode in the preschool and primary grades toward the information specialist mode in the middle and upper grades.

This book is intended to help practitioners carry some of their pied piper activities into the middle and upper grades, to develop with teachers some instructional consulting partnerships based on a healthy mix of the aesthetic and the efferent, of literature and life, of work and play, and of the inner as well as outer worlds of personal reality. Finally, the book portrays a school community whose values, interpersonal relationships, and social interactions are models to which all professionals may aspire, regardless of their particular circumstances.

ELEANOR R. KULLESEID
Series Editor

PART 1

Thematic Exploring:
The Scenario for Adventure

Once I went on a vacation to the Birdseed Hotel. I got all my clothes packed and when I got there, I heard "Bok! Bok! Bok!" I saw a turkey running across the hall and I saw a chicken coming out of room 103. I said "holy cow" and the chicken said, "You mean 'holy bird'." Then I went to the bathroom and there was a duck sitting in the sink. (Daniel Fraidstern, age 10)

Peering into the Manhattan Country School Library, one might see a nine-year-old girl painting a sign with small precise strokes. The sign reads "Animalville." A pronounced buzz fills the library. Two girls dressed as insects, wearing large antennae, are practicing a magic trick with a disappearing handkerchief.

In the little kids' reading room a sign reads "Birdseed Hotel." One boy is setting up the hotel restaurant, arranging menus and goldfish crackers. A second boy, dressed as an ostrich, is breakdancing to the "Nutcracker Suite." A third boy is at the reception desk writing something in a guest book. Beside him are three pieces of fake cardboard luggage, a bell, and a box of hand-painted buttons with appropriate slogans (see fig. 1).

Near the reference section, a boy dressed as a dragon practices swishing his five-foot-long green construction paper tail. He is concentrating hard. A sign on the wall reads "Puff's Dragon Academy." Another sign announces the courses being taught: 1. Tail-Swishing. 2. Fire-Breathing. 3. Knight-Frying. A third sign gives the lyrics to a song. "Knights have slayed us, dinosaurs have betrayed us. But we still believe in the ancient dragon way." (Michael Klein, age 10) The librarian wanders around speaking calmly. "Good sign. They'll like that."

Three boys are setting up a cardboard highway. This is the Gibbon Driving School. Their car is called the Bananamobile. The driving rules are listed on a poster.

1. No climbing out of the window.
2. No reading the *Gorilla Gazette* while driving.
3. No monkeying around with the brakes.
4. No beating your chest on the highway.
5. No throwing your banana peels on the street.

Fig. 1. Animalville Buttons (Steven Escobar and Corinna Mantlow, age 11). Used with permission

Two children dressed in black and white fabric costumes rehearse their penguin walk with exaggerated feet and stiff, waddling movements. "Too fast. You're going too fast," says one. There is a flurry of last minute preparations. "Here come the little kids," someone announces. The librarian moves in to give certain groups some extra support.

"Hi!" welcomes one of the insects as the first and second graders begin to enter. "This is Animalville, and it is a very funny town. Look around. You're going to meet an ostrich and some penguins. You might even meet a dragon, but he won't hurt you."

It is not unusual for the library at Manhattan Country School to be transformed into an Animalville or a Camelot or a Wild West town. The library is perceived as an imagination center and laboratory where different age groups can come together and share an adventure through thematic exploring.

A Definition of Thematic Exploring

Thematic exploring is an approach to library curriculum in which a variety of dramatic and expressive activities evolve from a central theme, topic, or idea selected by the library media specialist, often in cooperation with one or more teachers. Animalville, for example, was the culminating activity of a thematic exploring unit on humor. In such a process, students are introduced to the theme and, with teachers' guidance, begin to interpret it in-depth with a strong sense of adventure. Collaborative planning and implementation are major components of thematic exploring, and require the ability to improvise, to shift course. The library media specialist and teachers will have definite learning objectives in mind, but the schedule of planned activities may take an unexpected or new direction, depending on the circumstances.

Similar to the webbing framework developed by Charlotte Huck and her colleagues, thematic exploring is also a way of integrating literature experiences with language arts and other content area topics.[1] Class activities often draw from a common childhood literary heritage of folklore and fairy tales. Connections are often made between two different classes and age groups in developing the units, which usually span a period of some weeks. They often culminate in a public event that allows older students to function as teachers for younger classes, or the whole school community. Whatever the particular content may be, at the conclusion of such a unit teachers and children feel as if they have been on an exciting journey together.

A Framework for Thematic Exploring

Many possible routes are available for the journeys suggested and illustrated in this book. The planning is always based on a combination of variables: curricula content and sequence, age and developmental level of students involved, the group's style of social interaction and learning needs, teachers' objectives and interests, and the library media specialist's objectives. Although thematic exploring units may develop differently and, as in a journey, plans may be subject to change, they do have in common an underlying sequential and conceptual framework (see fig. 2).

Steps	Activities
1. Choose the theme	Assess student/teacher agendas through dialogues, discussions
2. Plan the journey	Work out calendar with teachers, collect materials
3. Begin the journey	Create the mood, excite curiosity, present the literary lure
4. Take some excursions	Reading, writing, listening, speaking, drawing, acting, singing
5. Celebrate the journey	Choose format, plan and execute with students and teachers, invite guests, enjoy

Fig. 2. A Sequential Framework for Thematic Exploring

The journey begins with conversation, as those involved decide on a theme and a way of exploring. Choosing a theme is an important matter, for it must be exciting and relevant for children to connect personally. The theme should arouse curiosity and raise questions. Those aspects explored should be age-appropriate and in harmony with children's developmental and learning needs. The theme should also be universal, helping children see that they are part of the global community.

The starting point can be anything—a game, a poem, a story, a magic trick— and often comes from unexpected sources. For example, one group's excitement about the lizard band in Daniel Pinkwater's *Lizard Music* inspired the creation of the humor unit, which led to the Animalville celebration. Whatever the stimulus, it should involve children immediately and touch a personal chord. The library media specialist creates a mood in which everyone feels relaxed and focused, in which there is a sense of fun and promise of adventure.

There should be an openness about the way the journey moves. It depends on the nature of the group. What sparks the members? What are their strengths? What are their interests? What are their concentration skills? What are their social dynamics? A particular group may have strong scientific leanings. Another group may be enthusiastic about drama and poetry.

Much also depends on the personality, strengths, and educational goals of the teachers with whom the library media specialist plans the journey. The library media specialist must have an understanding of the school community to know who might be open to this kind of exploring. Not everyone will immediately appreciate the serious learning that goes into the creation of an Animalville. At the beginning, only a few teachers might see the potential of various themes for integration with curriculum content areas.

As guide on the journey, the library media specialist should listen carefully to group members and be prepared to move in many different directions. If the journey is planned to the last detail, there will be no unknown areas, and perhaps little surprise or discovery. The process may then become a matter of strictly adhering to a formula.

Enough time must be set aside for a number of excursions that lengthen or vary the journey. Ideally, six to eight sessions are needed to give thematic exploring richness and depth. This piece of time can become very defined and have a strong and unique character. "Remember the spring of the elves?" "Remember the winter of the pirates?" The journey will evoke many feelings and images for children. Time seems suspended when something cumulative and powerful happens, whereas, all too often in teaching, time is rushed and fragmented.

Sessions should be varied, allowing children to explore the theme through many types of excursions: reading, storytelling, dramatic play, puppetry, creative writing, art, music, movement, field study, interviewing, and other kinds of research. Some of the exploring is individual and personal; some exploring might involve pairs of children, small groups, or an entire class. Other resource people—special teachers, parents, community members—might be involved as well.

The journey culminates in a celebration that integrates aspects of the exploring and allows everyone to contribute his or her individual gifts. Someone might want to compose music. Someone might like to illustrate signs and posters. A format may be chosen by the library media specialist, or it may be developed in planning sessions with children and teachers. "How can we share our learnings and excitement with others in the school?" The celebration might take the form of an imaginary world, a banquet or a festival. There is something quite magical about creating a world together. Everyone is needed. Everyone can help. The library becomes transformed through the collaborative power of young imaginations.

An Account of the Process for Developing One Journey

Many ways of mapping a journey are available, depending on the participants, the time of year, the curriculum, and other variables. The following description of a unit on "Caravan and Marketplace" illustrates how these journeys can evolve.

1. *Choose the theme.* One of the social studies units in the sixth grade centers on ancient China. The classroom teacher, art teacher, and library media specialist began to brainstorm about possible themes and projects. They looked at ways the library and art programs could enrich this study by enabling children to feel the soul of traditional Chinese culture through explorations of music, art, and literature. Since this thematic study was curriculum-generated, the challenge was to link the historical content to children's interests and developmental needs. They decided to focus on the idea of the marketplace in order to tap into sixth graders' strong interest in monetary matters and their excitement about shopping and being consumers. Such a theme could also help them learn about the value of work and the need to acquire certain skills and tools of technology.

2. *Plan the journey.* During the next few weeks, the teachers and library media specialist collected materials that might help give children a clearer, deeper, more visual sense of ancient China. They found maps, folktales, poetry, reproductions of paintings. They contacted and cultivated human resources: Asian-American parents, members of New York's Chinatown community. They juggled and reorganized schedules so that they could teach together and have extended blocks of times. They continued to meet and share works that moved and stimulated them. They began to crystallize their plans and talk about possible excursions.

3. *Begin the journey.* The library media specialist used a classical music selection "In a Persian Market" (Ketèlbey) as the starting point for the children's entry into the process. Students were asked to conjure up whatever images they could while listening to the piece. After distributing paper and drawing materials, he asked students to draw some of their images. The music seemed to evoke interest and energy. Their drawings were quite animated, with elephants, camels, and women with pottery. There was already a feeling of festivity in many of the drawings.

Then he asked the students to imagine being visitors to this marketplace. Together they described the myriad of sights, sounds, and aromas. They speculated about some of the human dramas that might occur: a child getting lost, an argument over the price of a fabric. They considered how the marketplace was a setting where information and stories were exchanged and where gossip and intrigue could flourish. Students compared the old marketplace with the shopping mall of today. How were they similar? How were they different? They decided that the economic functions were the same and that both served as gathering places. They felt, though, that the old marketplaces of their imaginings were more personal and unique, compared with the interchangeable and less exciting modern malls.

4. *Take some excursions.* Children scoured the library and the classroom for information on Chinese traditions and institutions. They researched day-to-day living conditions, the larger historical context, and the arrival of Marco Polo and other Europeans. In the art program they visited museums to see Chinese works of art and other cultural artifacts. They also planned in detail and created a strikingly ornate

mural depicting a caravan traveling in Asia, bearing baskets of fruits and gifts. Chinese folktales were read aloud during library periods. Students discussed what truths were being imparted and whether these truths were always valid. Working in small groups, the children then dramatized some of these tales. In a creative writing session, children imagined themselves as Europeans witnessing the sights of ancient China for the first time. They described their impressions:

As I walked through the sparkling, magical gates, I felt as though I were in heaven. I saw women walking with beautiful hair, wearing delicate robes with exquisite designs. The robes were made of the softest material ever. (Kim Conroy, age 12)

As I walked closer to the Emperor, I saw all his guards and helpers parading before him. At the back of the procession were all his loyal followers who wished to be seen with him. All wore extravagent kimonos made of silk with nightingales embroidered on the backs of them. (Brian Greenbush, age 11)

As we entered China, I saw a man flying a kite of all different colors, and it looked in a way as if it were floating in the sky, gliding in the wind. I saw a group of children learning how to dance, and the women teaching them were so beautiful and graceful, it made me feel heavy-footed and clumsy. (Anne Woodman, age 12)

5. *Celebrate the journey.* The library media specialist held a series of planning sessions with the teachers, various small groups of children, and sometimes the entire class. They finally decided to try to recreate an old Chinese marketplace. Working in pairs, sixth graders searched for information about the kinds of merchants, buyers, priests, and entertainers who would inhabit this market. Time was spent creating costumes, making props, working out words and ploys to attract customers. Centers and booths were set up and given flavor through visual touches.

The first and second grade group was chosen for the audience because these six- and seven-year-olds still had a strong sense of wonder, and so enjoyed the pleasures of make-believe. They had, in fact, studied the modern produce marketplace in their "city" curriculum. There was also a considerable age difference between them and the sixth graders; the older kids would feel more confident and less inhibited.

Some sixth graders helped to create the caravan that would lead the younger ones to the marketplace. The caravan would be the lure to set the tone and invite the children on the journey. The older kids made cloth and cardboard animals and worked out small theatrical vignettes to further entice the younger group.

At last, after six weeks of researching, planning, and creating, the caravan was brought to life. The sixth graders began their processional to the first/second grade classroom. Costumed as merchants and entertainers, they entered dramatically with drums beating and incense burning. The science teacher, Leena, led the dancing, wearing bracelets and bells. There were colorful horses and a nightingale in a gold cage. The caravan would stop from time to time, as it circled around, so the children could hear the pleas of a beggar, the flute song of a musician, and a merchant haggling with his camel:

> Oh, no! Don't stop now. We only have one mile. How about a bale of hay? Or do you want a nudge? Okay, I'll give you a bale of hay. I'll give you two bales of hay. Come on, I know that you're tired. How about two bales of hay, some water, and one of my rings. (Sam Pott, age 11)

The younger kids looked amused as the spice merchant Tinnamon boasted about his "cloves, garlic and cinnamon." Several children petted the seven-foot dragon and someone mischievously pulled on the elephant's tail. The children were then invited to follow the caravan. Eagerly they approached the doorway of the sixth grade classroom, glimpsing the mural and smelling the fragrance of thyme. Once inside, they encountered the richly textured world of a market-place—a world of beggars, barterers, and magical entertainers.

In this exciting world they could try out different kinds of teas: morning tea, after-dinner tea, or tea for special occasions. The tea merchant was polite and never pushy. They could experiment with chopsticks and sample delicious delicacies made by three chefs. It was hard to choose among two kinds of pasta and three kinds of rice.

They could learn to make actual kites from the kitemakers, and "see paper and wood fly like birds and glide in the wind." They could learn from the royal mathematician how to use the abacus. "This amazing invention will help you to learn arithmetic and keep account of your belongings."

They could meet the turbaned snake charmer, hear him play his seductive tune, and witness the cobra rise out of his basket. They could watch the shadowmakers perform their exquisite dragon tale with shadow puppets, demonstrating the ancient art of China. They could then create their own shadow plays, and learn the secrets of the shadow world.

Afterwards, during the cleanup, the library media specialist could sense the pride and relief of the sixth graders. They had pulled it off, and now they felt empowered. They had bonded together and captured the spirit of the marketplace. As actors and teachers, they had transported the younger kids and themselves into another time and place. They had sustained it and made it believable.

Advantages of Thematic Exploring

Role Expansion

Thematic exploring offers library media specialists special opportunities for expanding and integrating the three professional roles described in *Information*

Power: information specialist, teacher, and instructional consultant.[2] Thematic exploring can make these roles more dynamic and give them breadth. It requires expertise to be an information specialist, providing students with access to resources as they do theme-related research for literary and historical contexts. The library media specialist must help the students interpret information gathered from many sources.

Thematic exploring requires the library media specialist, in the role of teacher, to help students develop criteria for evaluating information and the skills to become effective communicators in all the language arts—listening, talking, reading, writing. It facilitates teaching them about the production of media—live drama, pictures, slides, video, etc.—so they will have more options and modes for conveying their ideas and findings.

Thematic exploring offers the library media specialist informal opportunities to shape the role of instructional consultant, drawing teachers and administrators into planning and implementing activities, forging connections with the curriculum, and adding new instructional dimensions, as well as resources, to specific units. By asserting their roles as innovative leaders and literary pied pipers, library media specialists will be able to make powerful connections with students and staff members. The special projects that often conclude a study depend almost fully on the pooling of the strengths and energies of those who are involved; the richer the partnerships, the more buoyant the celebrations.

Some library media specialists may have reservations about trying out a more collaborative, open-ended kind of program. Thematic exploring is a risky process; once begun it involves full immersion, spontaneity, and often giving up control of the action. This "serious fun" can produce extraordinary results, though. By providing "more opportunities to develop the imaginative and playful potentials of their students more deeply and more widely," teachers and library media specialists may begin to see children and themselves in new and exciting ways.[3] Thematic exploring is one of the most effective vehicles for trying out the role of instructional consultant and establishing the library media specialist's presence in the school as a source of information, ideas, activities, and even delight.

Integration of Aesthetic and Cognitive Functions

Another important value of thematic exploring is that it combines cognitive and aesthetic functions within the information-skills curriculum, and motivates children to make quests for knowledge that are deeply meaningful and that move them personally. It offers opportunities to leaven the current emphasis on new information technologies with the traditional emphasis on pleasure reading and the enjoyment of literature. It suggests that information may be sought, accessed, analyzed, synthesized, and transmitted through narrative as well as expository forms.

Thematic exploring provides children with rich opportunities for hands-on concrete experiences, for more abstract thinking and problem solving, and for taking on the role of teacher or guide as they involve other students in the scenarios they have created. For example, "The pirate academy" was founded by nine- and ten-year-old students to help the librarian to bring the kindergarten/ grade one pirate study to an exciting finish. The academy is described as the culminating celebration in the Journey Log section of "Villains and Bullies," the first of five adventures found in Part 2 of this book. The younger children had been obsessed with pirates and had explored new areas of content: the workings of a ship, the dangers of the sea. They learned to speak a new language as they devoured new vocabulary words, chose pirate names, and hid treasure maps. There was so much to talk and write about. All kinds of episodes could be translated into stories. After this study the students couldn't wait to get their hands on pirate books. They identified strongly with the world they had created, and were always eager to relive and renew their buccaneering days. The link to pirates was personal and heartfelt.

A Common Literary Heritage

The frequent use of folk and fairy tales in thematic exploring helps to weave a child's home and school worlds together, rekindling the pleasures of early childhood bedtime rituals. The library media specialist can build on this common heritage of characters and events, of shared meanings and interpretations, stimulating students to rethink them with fresh developmental perspectives. The reworking of such archetypes as Cinderella and Pinocchio allows middle- and upper-grade students to create dramatic improvisations more readily, for they have grown up with these characters and know well their yearnings and their foibles. The repertoire of familiar figures should be expanded to include many different cultures, represented by such colorful characters as Anansi, the Hodja, and Juan Bobo. And children, as members of a universal multicultural stock company, should have chances to play many different parts—the hero, the heroine, the villain, the wizard, the fool.

Thematic exploring weaves together a number of familiar library-based functions and activities, including storytelling. The story worlds described in this book may be seen as expanded story circles where children and adults bring stories to life and become characters in many times and places. In the shared creation of a story there is the immediacy of eye-to-eye and voice-to-voice contact. There is an exchange of energy and a concern for poetic expression. This kind of sharing requires a trust between teller and listener, a sense of being safe within the bounds of the magic circle. Then, as the journey ensues, children are ready to adapt, to detour, to enter, and to explore even the darkest woods.

Guiding Principles

The following sections of Part 1 provide a more extended educational rationale that examines thematic exploring from three broad perspectives: social development, psychological development, and literacy development. These perspectives represent core beliefs about learning and growth; they form the basis for the choice of themes and the process by which they are implemented. They also embody goals to which educators universally subscribe. One is the development of social values in terms both of individual ethics and of collective responsibility for membership in a learning community. The second is the acknowledgment of children as thinking and feeling beings and as active, not passive, learners. Students flourish when they are offered developmentally appropriate activities and content, and when they can exercise some measure of control over the course of learning. The third is the development of powerful communication skills and attitudes gained through the acquisition and use of literacy and literature, and a desire to use them in pursuit of lifelong learning and pleasure. These three perspectives are the guiding principles for thematic exploring.

Notes

1. Charlotte S. Huck et al., *Children's Literature in the Elementary School,* 4th ed. (New York: Holt, Rinehart and Winston, 1987), p. 653. *See also* issues of the quarterly journal, *The WEB,* coedited by Huck and Janet Hickman, published by Ohio State University.

2. American Assn. of School Librarians and Assn. for Educational Communications and Technology, *Information Power: Guidelines for School Library Media Programs* (Chicago: American Library Assn.; Washington, D.C.: Assn. for Educational Communications and Technology, 1988), pp. 26–39.

3. David E. Purpel, *The Moral and Spiritual Crisis in Education: A Curriculum for Social Justice and Compassion in Education* (Westport, Conn.: Bergin and Garvey, 1988), p. 136.

Reference

Pinkwater, Daniel Manus. *Lizard Music.* Putnam, 1976.

Social Perspectives

Educators, parents, and legislators have always acknowledged the importance of the school as an agent for socialization. In these turbulent times, the locus of responsibility for social and moral education seems to be shifting from the dinner table to the cafeteria, and from church and synagogue to the classroom. The school community may well become the primary group from which students will derive their identity both as individuals and as group members. Individual teachers have always been mentors and models for children; today their collective behavior as members of an interactive learning community can have a powerful impact on the development of students' concepts of membership in community and society. Those responsible for improving students' achievement scores in individual classrooms are being urged to take more responsibility for a vision of the school as a democratic community, even knowing that "much of our culture teaches us not the skills of community building but rather of individual competition."[1]

Competition versus Community

How can adults help children learn to be caring and collaborative? What happens when children are too often presented with competitive models in school? "This is the best third grade class." "I know we can win this contest!" Even if students don't see their teachers competing, they may seldom see them engaged in warm, sustained, purposeful interactions. Many schools are conditioned to using competition to ensure motivation and interest, to spur children on with the promise of an external reward. In these situations students can become fiercely single-minded, seeking only bottom line results—a win, a final grade, one teacher's judgment.

Competition can have a heat and intensity that can close things off and cause children to feel insecure and withdrawn. Competition can foster aggressiveness and one-upmanship, or it can foster despair. "Unfortunately, most students perceive school as predominantly a competitive enterprise. They either constantly

12

work hard in school to do better than the other students, or they take it easy because they do not believe they have a chance to win.''[2]

Educators, as well as children, need nurture and support opportunities for informal interaction as members of a school community. If teachers are to become powerful change agents in this area, they need to be visibly connected, communicating, planning, building with one another. Ideally, the community of the school should matter as much as the teacher's individual classroom. In schools where participative staff decision making is cultivated, teachers are likely to be more invested, to feel a deeper sense of belonging. Educators who deal cooperatively with issues of student concerns, curriculum, personnel, and working conditions can more clearly understand the school's mission, knowing that they have the power to change its direction.

They are challenged to solve problems and be innovative, to look toward themselves in the search for solutions. But such empowerment and understanding does not happen overnight. "Ways have to be found to give teachers experiences in working together so they can begin to see how other adults can be important to them.''[3]

Community Building through Thematic Exploring

The building of a cooperative, compassionate, and intellectually invigorating school community is everyone's responsibility. Leadership is shared; at various times anyone might emerge to provide a vision, act as a catalyst and coordinator of a curriculum initiative, a special event, a new program. Library media specialists are in the perfect position to exercise leadership, and to initiate or strengthen their instructional consulting role through thematic exploring. They have a unique perspective in the school, an encompassing view of personalities, teaching styles, and agendas. They can have potential contact with every member of that community—teacher, child, parent, administrator. They are actively involved in many facets of the total school curriculum. They know what individuals and groups can contribute, and which groups might mix most effectively. They have knowledge, resources, and a belief that program excellence is founded on cooperation.

> An effective school library media program depends on the collaborative efforts of all those who are responsible for student learning. . . . In effect, all members of the educational community, including teachers, principals, students, and library media specialists, become partners in a shared goal—providing successful learning experiences for all students.[4]

Literacy events that emanate from the library media program can foster powerful partnerships between students and teachers in different classes and between staff members and administrators in the school community. Thematic exploring, in particular, brings different ages together in flexible and imaginative ways. Teachers are learners; students are teachers. Remarkable changes can occur when students plan the courses of study for a pirate academy or create an old Chinese marketplace. Working with younger children can allow older ones to express their gentle sides. It can free them from their peers for a time. It can enable them to be models and to be admired. Children nourished on these types of adventures learn the languages of improvisation and collaboration. They experience the pleasures of both individual and collective achievement as working group members engaged in a special kind of theatrical play.

As director of the "play," the library media specialist needs to nourish the actors and discover their secret skills or hobbies. "Do you sing?" "Do you play the harmonica?" Teachers, too, like to have their special aspects of self revealed and celebrated. They begin to enjoy these opportunities in which they can enter new roles, play with other actors, and not feel so isolated. Seeing their teachers in this light, revealing their playfulness, gives license to children to take risks. It also conveys to them that these activities are important. During the past seven years, students at Manhattan Country School have enjoyed the following gallery of performances: Gloria, the nurse-receptionist, reigning as Queen of the Renaissance Faire; Toni, the teacher of five- and six-year-olds, as a balking cow refusing to give milk at the County Fair; Jane, the teacher of six- and seven-year-olds, dressed as Esmerelda, the magician's daughter, presenting her mystifying "secret object" trick; Junius, the teacher of seven- and eight-year-olds, bellowing as the wolf in an improvised opera version of *Little Red Riding Hood;* Lois, the lower school head, square dancing in raucous style at the Wild West saloon; Cynthia, the fifth grade teacher, dazzling her students as one of the "Supremes" during Time Machine week; David, the sixth grade teacher, in pirate regalia, hiding in a tree in Central Park; Chris, the eighth grade advisor, as a razzle-dazzle producer chomping on his cigar during play auditions.

Even the youngest four- and five-year-olds can be involved in school events as both participants and initiators. Once, after responding to their enthusiasm for the book *Chicken Little* (Kellogg), the author suggested that they trick the people of the school and convince them that the sky was falling. The fours and fives, assisted by spelling experts from the sixth grade, made over forty signs that conveyed this cosmic predicament. ("Stay Indoors!" "Henny Penny says, 'Be Careful!' ") (see fig. 3)

Secretly, in small groups, they dispersed these signs all over the school. They slipped one under the science room door during a lecture. They posted another in the lost and found area. Of course there was a bit of commotion as people began to notice the signs. Everyone in the school became involved warning each other, taking precautions. The reading specialist wore her umbrella all afternoon. Some of the administrators walked around in exaggerated dismay. Everyone was going

Fig. 3. Chicken Little Warning Sign (anonymous five-year-old artist and sixth grade speller). Used with permission

along with the joke. The children indeed felt enormous pleasure from their triumph. They had honored Henny Penny and Foxy Loxy. They had gone on secret
missions. They had tickled the funny bone of the school. They also proved that
the school was, indeed, a true social community—one in which there was the
presence of a common understanding and shared interpretation of events,
themes, and metaphors as presented in a literary canon of folktales and stories
familiar to all community members.

Group Power

Thematic exploring both illustrates and exemplifies the power of the small-
group learning experience. Children of mixed abilities establish a common
purpose and common goals as they plan and implement projects together.
They become keenly aware of how groups work, and how each person oper-
ates in the group. They develop interpersonal skills and a sense of shared
responsibility. Striking attitudinal changes take place as they become more
sensitive to their partners and more committed to the partnerships. "How can
I help?" "What can I do next?" They learn to be flexible, cooperative, and to
value the individual strengths of each member. They derive pleasure from
playing off each other and from simply engaging in a dynamic, creative process. Hopefully, they will "acquire the ability to use their knowledge and
resources in collaborative activities with other people in their careers, families, communities, and the larger society."[5] The collaborative, rather than
competitive, child may be the one best prepared for tomorrow's global community. It is this child who can see a broad range of possibilities for communicating ideas and discoveries. It is this child who, with generosity and adapt-
ability, can draw out the strengths of others and who can play diverse roles,
including leader, listener, and negotiator.

Multicultural Awareness

The emphasis on dramatic play and dramatizations allows children to experiment
with roles, step outside themselves, and experience the world from different
points of view. Living inside so many characters can help them to be more
empathetic. Literature sharing can lead to greater appreciation of individual differences. Children are volatile, often changing their perceptions, loyalties, and
alliances. They may identify with many groups, not just their cultural group. In-
depth discussions about what motivates a character can provide insights and
foster attitudes of acceptance and tolerance. They will perhaps learn to probe
deeper when examining the behavior of others, and not judge so quickly or
harshly.

Children also need to learn that words and pictures can sting, that books and films presenting offensive portraits of groups can cause embarrassment. Stereotyping can prevent children from seeing the complexity of others.

Thematic exploring can include a consideration of censorship issues. Why are books like *In the Night Kitchen* (Sendak) and *Catcher in the Rye* (Salinger) considered dangerous by some people? Who are those who sit in judgment? What are their qualifications and biases? How can textbooks be slanted? How do historical works sometimes distort the facts? Why are the contributions of particular groups sometimes ignored?

Self-image is another important social perspective. How might a child feel whose group is written about, when a particular book is read aloud by the teacher or librarian? Will the child feel recognition and pride, or discomfort and hurt? In a picture book, do the characters and settings seem natural or contrived? Are the main characters in a chapter book unique and textured, having both strengths and weaknesses? Could knowing these characters, through reading the book, expand someone's awareness of that group in a positive way? What is the tone of the book? Is it pedantic? Is it patronizing?

One doesn't always need to turn away from a book if there are objections to it. The library media specialist may want to elaborate on a book's historical context as part of a thematic exploring unit. He or she may want to open things up when introducing a work, raising issues of controversy right at the beginning. For example, he or she could present a book such as *Stevie* (Steptoe) written in first person dialect, and have older children discuss their responses to it. Does the dialect impede their pleasure or understanding of the story? Could it cause someone to feel uncomfortable? They could examine the illustrations in *The Five Chinese Brothers* (Bishop) to see why many people consider them stereotypical and harmful. Some children might then want to create their own drawings. So much depends on the sensitivity of the group and the kind of trust the library media specialist has built with each member.

Ethical Judgment

Such experiences help students to see how social justice and equality issues come up in the storybook world as well as the real world. They could then begin to focus on the questions they ask so often: "Why are people poor?" "Why do people hurt one another?" "Why are there wars?" Do individuals have the right to be different? If this is so, why are certain members of the community often threatened by those who do not conform? What are the rights of minorities? How have these rights evolved? What are the rights of people who have recently immigrated here? What are the rights of the homeless? Who are their advocates?

Thematic exploring should also offer opportunities for children to consider their legacies to future generations, to understand that they are accountable to those who follow. Will they fight effectively to conserve clean air and water? Will they combat the illegal dumping of waste products? Will they help alleviate conditions of poverty and hunger? Will they seek to create a more humanistic society?

Children must be given the opportunity to examine such issues in-depth because they will be asked to make moral choices, and the choices they make as individuals will have considerable impact on their society. How will they respond to pressure? How will they come to recognize subtle forms of injustice? How can adults equip them to view situations objectively, to take a stand, and to express dissent? Can adults teach children to be passionate about ideas, but dispassionate when discussing them, and to avoid becoming rigid and self-righteous?

Children need to become aware of "the different ultimate sources for morality, including religion." They must have something to draw upon, some kind of guidelines or ethical framework. In confronting these concerns, the Association for Supervision and Curriculum Development's Panel on Moral Education defines the morally mature person as one who: "(1). Respects human dignity; (2). Cares about the welfare of others; (3). Integrates individual interests and social responsibilities; (4). Demonstrates integrity; (5). Reflects on moral choices; (6). Seeks peaceful resolution to conflict."[6] Some educators may challenge this set of criteria and argue about the semantics, but it does provoke inquiry and offers an urgently needed point of departure for debate.

In the illuminating and powerful book, *The Moral and Spiritual Crisis in Education: A Curriculum for Social Justice and Compassion in Education,* David E. Purpel envisions an education "directed toward a loving, compassionate and just world," where all people are linked by a "common history of struggle." Purpel writes with vigor about those extraordinary teachers who generated hope, transcended time and place, and changed human consciousness. Teachers such as Moses, Jesus, Gandhi, and Martin Luther King, Jr., were compelled to take dangerous risks because of their tenacity and clarity of vision. Their beliefs affirmed "the quality of human life and the importance of human freedom."[7]

Cultural Heroes as Moral Models

Moral issues are implicitly addressed through the process of thematic exploring, and they often become the primary focus of content, as in the theme of heroes introduced by the library media specialist and teacher to a fifth grade class. Through numerous discussions and debates they began to wrestle with criteria for defining a hero. Must a hero be intelligent? Must a hero have great physical strength? Must a hero be self-sacrificing? Must a hero overcome handicaps?

Does a hero always have a vision? Must a hero inspire, uplift, and help alleviate the hardships of others? They considered whether heroes—the Mandelas of South Africa, Lech Walesa of Poland, Sakharov of Russia, Cesar Chavez of the United States—only emerged in times of crises and oppression.

Fifth graders interviewed parents and other adults to identify the heroes that they had grown up with and find out what they admired about them. Some of these heroes were personal—teachers who had inspired them and nurtured their talents, and family members who had risked their lives and escaped from totalitarian worlds. Some parents mentioned fictional heroes (Robin Hood, Scarlett O'Hara) and biographical heroes (Anne Frank, Claude Brown).

The students asked themselves why people need heroes. They decided that heroes might be needed to speak for people, and rescue them, to lighten the dark and even ease the boredom. Heroes as role models can set standards of excellence to which others can aspire. Heroes such as Helen Caldicott can articulate the concerns of many (the effects of nuclear holocaust) and present a case that is both enlightening and forceful.

Why do people idealize heroes and refuse to see them in human terms? Why do people fail to accept and recognize their flaws? How do biographies sometimes contribute to this? What are some historical incidents that have involved fallen idols (the Black Sox Scandal, Watergate)? Why do these events shake people so, and cause them to feel betrayed?

Who are the unknown heroes, the collective heroes (French resistance fighters, labor organizers, civil rights activists)? Those engaged in the Underground Railroad, for example, took incredible, life-threatening risks. Their acts reflected their daring and compassion, but they received no awards and have mostly remained nameless. They were perhaps buoyed by their concerns for a more just society and were willing to take stands that set them apart from popular thinking.

In thematic exploring projects such as the hero study, children engage continually in a process of give and take. They are encouraged to explore difficult questions, to share ideas and feelings, and to clarify their own experiences, often through creative writing and drama. As they dramatized the lives of American folk heroes (John Henry, Mike Fink, Annie Oakley), the fifth graders were allowed collectively to take charge and feel a sense of competency and power. As collaborators they could move farther than they ever could on their own as individuals. They could flounder and get stuck and still count on the support and energy of others. They had a direct experience of a cooperative group that can organize, build, and have impact through its collective power. In the future these same children may come to see themselves as problem solvers, activists, and initiators who have impact within the context of a broader global community. Many of the metaphors for thought and action will have come from the literary sources they have interpreted through the vehicle of thematic exploring.

Notes

1. David E. Purpel, *The Moral and Spiritual Crisis in Education: A Curriculum for Social Justice and Compassion in Education* (Westport, Conn.: Bergin & Garvey, 1988), p. 127.

2. David W. Johnson et al., *Circles of Learning: Cooperation in the Classroom* (Alexandria, Va.: Assn. for Supervision and Curriculum Development, 1984), p. 2. *See also* Robert E. Slavin et al., eds., *Learning to Cooperate, Cooperating to Learn* (New York: Plenum, 1985).

3. Ron Brandt, "Teacher Empowerment: A Conversation with Ann Lieberman," *Educational Leadership* 46:25 (May, 1989).

4. *Information Power,* p. 21f.

5. Johnson, *Circles of Learning,* p. 7.

6. Assn. for Supervision and Curriculum Development, Panel on Moral Education, "Moral Education in the Life of the School," *Educational Leadership* 45:5 (May, 1988).

7. Purpel, *Moral and Spiritual Crisis,* p. 123.

References

Bishop, Claire H. *The Five Chinese Brothers.* Coward, 1938.

Kellogg, Steven. *Chicken Little.* Morrow, 1983.

Salinger, J. D. *Catcher in the Rye.* Little, 1981.

Sendak, Maurice. *In the Night Kitchen.* Harper, 1970.

Steptoe, John. *Stevie.* Harper, 1969.

Developmental
Perspectives

Educational reform in the eighties has evoked many of the ideas introduced by a progressive educational reform movement founded nearly a century ago. In 1897 John Dewey cautioned practitioners that "—this educational process has two sides—one psychological and one sociological—and that neither can be subordinated to the other, or neglected, without evil results following. Of these two sides the psychological is the basis. The child's own instincts and powers furnish the material and give the starting-point for all education."[1]

Dewey's philosophy has been supported by a large and growing body of research that has had significant impact on educators' attitudes and practices. For one thing, educators are trying to become more aware of the needs and strengths of individual students. They know that each person learns differently and comes to the learning situation with unique feelings, attitudes, experiences, and skills. Developmental psychologists like Howard Gardner have created interesting and complex theories of multiple types of intelligence.[2] These ideas are also linked to the research on individual learning styles, much of which has been been interpreted for practitioners by the Dunns and others, who challenge teachers to provide students with multisensory and multimedia learning opportunities.[3] Innovative educational programs have stressed the importance of moving away from the large, impersonal factory model of schooling toward the model of a small-scale community of learners, creating environments that allow individual students with diverse backgrounds and needs to flourish.[4]

Developmental factors are important in choosing books and films that are both satisfying and age-appropriate for children. The same is true for developing a curriculum unit; the topics, materials, and instructional strategies for thematic exploring must have the same integrity. The most vital themes touch the core in children, building on their genuine interests and acknowledging their real concerns. This is why certain themes can be so inviting and why children become so deeply absorbed while exploring them. The theme of "river journeys," for example, appeals to the yearning part of a child, the dream part. People of all ages have wanted to sail away at times, to simply follow a creek or see what is around the bend. In *Paddle-to-the-Sea* (Holling), children identify strongly with the lovingly carved canoe, feeling wistful and urgent as this model boat journeys to the ocean. Children who feel trapped and confined can feel a definite release as they become transported by the power of the story. The theme of ''quests'' appeals to children's desires to be heroic. This might explain the popularity of the *Indiana Jones* movies and some of the Marvel comic books. So many day-to-day life experiences can cause children to feel small and impotent. Starring as the hero in a dramatized Greek myth can counterbalance some of these negative moments and help children to surge and be victorious. The theme might also help children see the value of having a goal and pursuing it, even when there are difficult obstacles to overcome. When children of a certain age group are drawn to a theme, it is important to think carefully about the content and nature of the journey these students are about to undertake. Are they ready for such an exploration? Are they trusting of you and of each other? What is the group's attention span? Will a discussion idea be too abstract? Will a project make children feel rushed or overstimulated? When they embark on a scary adventure, how can the library media specialist make them feel protected so they know they won't be stuck ''out there''?

What are the physiological concerns? Is eye-hand coordination sufficiently developed for a given activity to be undertaken with the hope of success? Choosing the right materials (for example, size of crayons, kind of scissors) can be a crucial factor in determining whether a project will be challenging or just frustrating. An understanding of developmental theories helps adults see what children might be coping and struggling with at various stages, and to be more aware of what they are learning and attempting to master. It provides general parameters of behavior, a developmental framework against which the library media specialist may assess the appropriateness and success of their adventures with language in the library media center.

Developmental Models

The developmental stage theories of Erik Erikson and Jean Piaget are the most quoted and best known to American educators. Erikson's model focuses on the psychodynamic development of the child within a social context, in relationship to others.[5] He identifies a sequence of increasingly complex stages, within each of which the child must resolve a basic life issue or developmental crisis before moving conflict-free into the next.

Jean Piaget's is a model of independent cognitive development; the child is viewed as a thinking and reasoning individual with an innate capacity to assimilate and synthesize fragmented perceptions into coherent concepts of reality.[6] The growing child moves from intuitive, concrete operations towards a more rational and abstract framework of knowledge based on logical operations.

Library media specialists have used these models in evaluating materials for inclusion in literature-based programs and as guides in helping teachers and students select age- and stage-appropriate materials.[7] The following sections, organized into three major childhood periods, mesh the developmental insights of Erikson and Piaget with a sample of the rich variety of literature found in library media center print and nonprint collections. Such literature can inspire and initiate a unit of thematic exploring.

Early Childhood: Birth to Seven Years

Erikson postulates two early childhood stages. The primary developmental challenge of the first stage is identified as autonomy versus doubt. From eighteen months to three years, children struggle to be independent without losing the security of loving parents. They often become engaged in a battle of wills in their wish to be omnipotent. They must learn to accept external control without being angry about it and, simultaneously, to develop the ability to control their internal impulses. They must become aware of their immediate world and of its inhabitants, including adults other than parents. They must come to terms with their own changing selves.

Initiative versus guilt poses the major developmental challenge in the second early childhood stage. Children from three to six years learn to be responsible for themselves and their toys. Their symbolic play is more complex and less concrete, with more evidence of fantasy. Yet they want to know how things work in the real world and use initiative to find things out. They learn that their behavior may at times be in opposition to the behavior of others and may feel a sense of guilt because of this.

Piaget also divides early childhood into two stages in the evolution of the child's thinking. In the preconceptual phase, two to four years, children's play centers on "how and why," and they have a strong interest in their immediate surroundings. They are very egocentric. They delight in the security of repetitive activities and routines. Yet they are beginning to engage in symbolic play. They can imagine an object to be something else; a block of wood can become a car or a bed.

Children in the period of intuitive thought, four to seven years, use chain reasoning, moving from particular to particular without generalizing. They are learning, through direct experiences, to become aware of cause and effect and to recognize differences between how things look and how they really are. They are just beginning to consciously distinguish fantasy from reality in stories, dreams, and in their everyday play. They are learning to become less egocentric. They are beginning to form reciprocal relationships with others.

A growing number of fine authors and illustrators have created picture books that reflect the needs and interests of children in this early childhood period. They are, in some respects, case studies of healthy development. For example, the young geographer in *The Line Up Book* (Russo) reveals many aspects of the first stages. He inventively uses familiar objects (blocks, books, bath toys) to create a path from his bedroom to the kitchen, but runs out of objects just before he reaches his goal. This book responds to the child's need to explore his own turf, to move through space, to identify, categorize, and manipulate objects of his home world and use them in the service of a special play activity. The child is pursuing his own agenda as mother makes her demands for his presence. The boy will get there, but on his own terms, demonstrating that he has successfully overcome doubt to achieve basic autonomy. And when he solves the problem he has set himself, the boy and his mother share a loving reunion, in which his initiative is rewarded with approval.

Mr. Gumpy's Outing (Burningham) addresses a child's fear about losing her balance and taking a tumble. "Will I fall down?" "Will the boat tip over?" The book appeals to a young child's sense of fantasy and playfulness and allows for her anticipation of events. It also requires some understanding of spatial relationships and of cause and effect to fully enjoy the comic predicament.

Sylvester and the Magic Pebble (Steig) recognizes a child's need to make wishes and engage in wishing rituals. Collecting pebbles helps Sylvester categorize and make sense of the world. When he discovers that he can cause magical events to occur with a crimson stone, it becomes his lucky piece. He feels powerful and protected. This humorous and scary yarn helps children confront the anxiety of being separated from parents. "What will happen to me?" It lets them fly loose with their imaginations and then brings them safely home, trusting that they will be reunited with parents at journey's end.

The Carrot Seed (Krauss) portrays a child coping with Erikson's stage-two issues by taking the initiative with determination, faith, and mastery. The child cares for his carrot seed even though no one thinks it will grow. He does specific things. He watches for signs. He waters it. When the carrot at last shoots out, he knows that he has persevered and made it happen. That is one of the reasons why children are so joyful in their response to this book.

In *Tigers in the Cellar* (Fenner), a child must come to terms with her own fantasies and fears as she prepares for bedtime. She can safely pretend to be a secret agent or a trapeze artist in her busy daytime life. At night, lying alone in the dark, she confronts and makes friends with the tigers of her imagination. When the girl tells her mom about her nocturnal adventures with the tigers, the mother's interpretation (distinguishing real from pretend) is not fully accepted. The reader is left to ponder the nature of creative fantasy. The products of human imagination have a reality of their own.

A book such as *Rain Makes Applesauce* (Scheer) enables children to delight in some of the pleasures of language: repetition, rhyming, and nonsense. They have learned what certain words mean and have begun the process of categorizing— naming the world and the objects in it. These intuitive thinkers also understand something about how things are supposed to work in the world. They are just beginning to distinguish sense from nonsense. Now they can play with words as objects of meaning and this makes them feel masterful. They see that sharing a joke is a way to make connections. "How silly!" they might react with amusement. "Elbows don't grow on a tickle tree." But, in fact, rain does make applesauce if you understand something about relationships, processes, and cause and effect. Hidden in the extravagant illustrations is a depiction of the growth cycle of plants and the seasons of the year that plants the nonsense in the soil of truth.

Middle Childhood: Seven to Eleven Years

During this period, children must deal with the developmental challenge identified by Erikson as industry versus inferiority. They are identified with the adult world and look to grownups as role models. Their need is to be productive and useful, and they feel pleasure in performing and completing tasks. It is a time when children may feel inadequate if they cannot show competence. Piaget describes this time as the period of concrete operations. Children move beyond one-dimensional thinking, and are learning to connect, conceptualize, and make simple generalizations. They are able to deal with chronology; they can remember the past, live in the present, and project future consequences of present action. Consequently, they can connect more deeply with story characters, with their motivations and causal relationships. They are able to process more complex and detailed information, and the desire to understand and master the real world may partially account for the great popularity of realistic fiction for this age group.

The main characters in the favorite series books (Ramona, Pippi Longstocking, The Great Brain, Cam Jansen, etc.) are competent and courageous. The title character in . . . *and now Miguel* (Krumgold) listens earnestly when his older brother teaches him how to catch a trout. Miguel can't wait to come of age, and his secret wish is to go with the men to take the sheep up the mountains. Eagerly, he seeks to bond with them and to assume the adult role.

The importance of having an adult role model is treated with both humor and sensitivity in *Danny: The Champion of the World* (Dahl). Danny worships his only parent, always seeking to emulate him. In all of their adventures (kite flying, poaching, midnight feasting), Danny learns the special ways and secret methods that will help him to be competent and resourceful. He learns to be excited by the challenges, to see possibilities. He can take the wild risks because he feels so loved.

Middle grade children are drawn to stories in which the main characters are struggling with feelings of loneliness and inadequacy. The film *J.T.* looks at a child whose fears cause him to withdraw. It offers a portrait of a sullen city boy who tunes out for good reason. He feels inadequate and ineffective in the world. His mother is always angry. He is failing at school. Neighborhood bullies continually threaten him and reinforce his sense of inferiority. When he finds a cat in an abandoned building, he is able to give, to express his warmth. The cat helps him to get outside of himself, and taking care of the cat makes him feel empowered.

The Eighteenth Emergency (Byars) elaborates on the powerful bully theme. When Mouse angers Hammerman, the school bully, he tries to use all of his wits and energy to avoid the inevitable showdown. Mouse's fear of Hammerman consumes and distracts him. Every outing becomes an ordeal. He starts to feel small and disgraced, embarrassed in his role as school victim. Everything else shrinks in importance, and this makes Hammerman a giant, ever omnipotent, always waiting in the wings. The author effectively uses humor to relieve the anxiety of Mouse's situation, and it is Mouse's own sense of humor that draws the reader to him and establishes empathy.

Bridge to Terabithia (Paterson) touches many children because it embraces so beautifully the concerns all children have. It looks at friendship and what draws individuals together. The story describes how the bond between Jesse Aarons and Leslie Burke deepens, even changing the way they view things. It shows the value of having a special place, a private kingdom where one can feel safe and powerful, and create one's own rules. It looks, too, at the possibility of death and the need to be remembered. This book asks children to think about their legacies.

The importance of friendships is a pivotal theme for middle graders. How does a person find a friend, establish common ground, and nurture the relationship? *The Noonday Friends* (Stolz) shows some of the pressures and insecurities that can tug at a friendship and threaten its stability. Franny and Simone have different responsibilities, different strengths and temperaments, different ways of interpreting events. Even their family dynamics contrast considerably. Franny's family members express anger in silences; Simone's family "battles around a great deal." Still, their friendship has durability. They are able to give and take, to bound back even after awkward, hurtful moments.

Jennifer, Hecate, Macbeth, William McKinley, and Me, Elizabeth (Konigsburg) explores how a friendship can infuse one's life with a sense of purpose and adventure. Elizabeth feels isolated until she meets up with Jennifer, "a self-proclaimed witch," and becomes her apprentice. They begin to share a rich and secret out-of-school bond as they perform magic chants and create magic potions. Their sealed blood pact becomes a source of power and trust, a kind of touchstone for all their adventuring. It is not surprising that children this age, feeling a lack of control and order in their world, are attracted by witchcraft or "Dungeons and Dragons" games. By mastering elaborate strategies, movements, rituals, and spells, a child can feel a deep sense of competence and adequacy.

Adolescence: Twelve to Twenty Years

The storms of adolescence are described by Erikson as the conflict between identity and role diffusion. This is a time when young people need to carve out their identity by separating from the family, and the peer group serves as a transitional family. It is a time of questioning adult authority; relationships to parents become threatened. Puberty triggers a loss of body identity, and sexual and aggressive drives become more intensified. In Piaget's model, the period of formal operations extends from eleven to fifteen years. Older children and adolescents can be deductive in their reasoning. They have an increased ability to link parts and wholes. They can evaluate the validity of information. They are more aware of relationships and can take another's point of view. They can, for instance, enter *Anne Frank: The Diary of a Young Girl* with a more developed world scheme. They are able to identify with a European culture in the 1940s. They are better able to grasp the idea of a world community in conflict.

Young adults are attracted to themes of survival. They can identify with someone who is struggling with the unknown as he or she moves on to the next stage of life. In *North to Freedom* (Holm), David has escaped from an East European prison and must invent and live by his own rules. He must lie still in times of light and then travel in the dark. He yearns for protection and guidance. When he loses his compass, he decides he must choose a god for himself, and creates a "God of Green Pastures." It is his way of sustaining hope and of addressing the things he cannot explain. Older readers can appreciate his struggle and renewal, his need to be cautious, and his learning to trust again.

In *The Witch of Blackbird Pond* (Speare), the spirited and rebellious Kit struggles to define herself and preserve her identity amongst members of a narrow-minded Puritan community. In dealing with so much fear and conformity, she begins to clarify her own values. *Annie John* (Kincaid) captures what a struggle adolescence can be, with its extraordinary mood swings. Annie is an island girl whose moods fluctuate often. She can immensely enjoy the irreverent doings of Friday afternoons, when she and her friends secretly "sing bad songs, use forbidden words," and show their various body parts. This contrasts with the deep melancholy she feels so intensely at other times. "It sat somewhere—maybe in my belly, maybe in my heart; I could not exactly tell—and it took the shape of a small black ball, all wrapped in cobwebs."[8] *Annie John* is about the sense of loss adolescents feel when their perceptions change, their bodies change, and they begin to move away from parents.

The Alfred Summer (Slepian) shows how the struggles of adolescents are compounded even more for those who have special needs. How can having cerebral palsy, for example, distort one's self-image and impede social relationships? Lester, the disabled hero of this novel, opens up considerably through his friendships with three other "misfits." He experiences a sense of belonging and is buoyed by the collective strength of the group. His anger starts to dissolve. He learns to trust, to even laugh at himself. He is more able to grasp the pain of his own family dynamic because now he has some distance.

The adolescent heroine in George Roy Hill's film, *The World of Henry Orient,* also fears that she is unwanted and unloved. She eases her pain through a series of escapades in which she and her friend spy on her pianist idol. This safe love interest allows her to fantasize and hope, and still remain in control.

Hallstrom's *My Life as a Dog* is a film so rich in layerings of emotion that it provides an abundance of material for thematic exploring. It foreshadows, in fact, most of the themes presented in Part 2 of this book. It looks at the theme of perceptions, how a child sees himself or herself and the world. Ingemar, a twelve-year-old Swedish boy with a dying mother and sometimes abusive brother, sees himself as a dog, unwanted and soon to be abandoned. His world has become a fearful place and his first-person narration is laced with statistics and references to casualties and tragic events. This is another survival tale. The young hero is trying to hold his world together, to keep a perspective, and to feel less diminished. "How will I make it in this world?" "Will I go hungry?" "Will I be loved?" "Where will I sleep?" The film examines, too, the powerful theme of nighttime and, in a climactic scene, reveals the boy's wave of anxiety when he locks himself in his uncle's summer house. His night fears have become uncontrollable and he is engulfed by a deep sense of loss and the fear that he will lose everything again. Ultimately, he finds a special place in his uncle's village and, with it, acceptance, warmth, a sense of belonging and community. The theme of humor is woven skillfully into the texture of the film, with the everyday humor of colorful village eccentrics like the neighbor on the roof, who goes for his annual bath outing in the village stream.

Sharing the same story with children at various stages of development can be exciting. What they bring—their concerns, their awareness of time and place, and their understanding of culture—will be quite different. Younger children listening to *Charlotte's Web* (White) can respond to its themes of friendship, loss and gain, and the life cycle. They can see the value of being resourceful and having a great idea. Older children can appreciate the intensity and nuances of the friendship, the depth of the language, the beauty of the pastoral setting. Revisiting fairy tales can be releasing for older children. They are no longer so frightened of witches and wolves. They can now confront and verbalize ideas of rage and oppression. They can examine these stories with strong feelings. They can understand the symbolism.

Making Connections with Students

Thematic exploring begins with knowing and understanding students as individuals; the curriculum grows from these roots. Building relationships with individual children means creating opportunities for spontaneous sharing, for laughter, and for serious conversation. There are numerous ways to open things up, to make personal, even playful connections with individual children. One interesting way to establish contact is to interview a student with a personal questionnaire.[9] Some years ago the author developed a "Favorite Things" questionnaire in a hospital play-therapy program. The results of these interviews would be posted on the beds of children. Doctors appreciated learning more about their young patients as interesting individuals, and were able to initiate real conversations with them.

Over the years this questionnaire has been modified and used in several school settings with great success. The librarian asks questions and writes down the responses. There are no right or wrong answers to these questions. The child being interviewed enjoys getting special attention, and the adult gets a better sense of what is unique about this student, what makes her or him "tick." The process is personal, bringing the adult and child together in a focused and relaxed way. What might the reader guess about the following children, on the basis of their interviews (see fig. 4)?

Marcus Arrington, age 8

color	blue
song	"Rock Island Line"
instrument	piano
way to travel	car
amusement ride	roller coaster
hiding place	"under my bed"
monster	Godzilla
toy	water gun
treasure	fifty cent piece
indoor game	I declare war
outdoor game	kickball
thing to wear	bluejeans
thing to make	brownies
thing to collect	coins
time of day	lunchtime
picture book	*Curious George*
chapter book	*James and the Giant Peach*
author	Roald Dahl
movie	*Legend*
fairy tale character	Jack (who climbed the beanstalk)
dinner	pizza
dessert	chocolate cake
drink	fruit punch
kind of store	pizza parlor
dream vacation place	Hawaii
month	February

Fig. 4. Favorite Things Questionnaire

Marcus Arrington, age 8

pet	Doberman pinscher
animal to be	tiger
secret power to have	invisibility
adventure	sleeping out at summer camp
wish	to do a triple flip in gymnastics
job to have	doctor
president	Washington
thing to do on Saturday	watch cartoons

Elvira Castillo, age 8

color	pink
song	"The Lion Sleeps Tonight"
instrument	piano
way to travel	airplane
amusement ride	water flume
hiding place	hall closet
monster	King Kong
toy	Cabbage Patch doll
treasure	seashell
indoor game	monopoly
outdoor game	baseball
thing to make	finger weavings
thing to collect	shells
thing to wear	long sleeved pink shirt
time of day	outside time ("going to the meadow")
picture book	*Sleeping Beauty*
chapter book	*Key to the Treasure*
author	Ann M. Martin
movie	*Oliver and Company*
fairy tale character	Cinderella
dinner	spaghetti
dessert	mint chocolate chip ice cream
drink	chocolate milk
kind of store	toy store
dream vacation place	a rain forest
month	April
pet	horse
animal to be	rabbit

Fig. 4—*Continued*

Elvira Castillo, age 8

secret power to have	to fly
adventure	climbing to the top of Bear Mountain
job to have	waitress
president	Washington
wish	"that my cat would stay alive forever"
thing to do on Saturday	watch television and go to the park

David Jiminez, age 9

color	light blue
song	"Nightmare on My Street"
instrument	recorder
way to travel	airplane
amusement ride	racing cars
hiding place	under bed
monster	Dracula
toy	Transformers
treasure	clock
indoor game	blackjack
outdoor game	soccer
thing to wear	grey jogging pants
thing to make	skateboards
thing to collect	Transformers
time of day	midnight
picture book	*Dr. DeSoto*
chapter book	*The Hobbit*
author	J. R. R. Tolkien
movie	*Big*
fairy tale character	Big Bad Wolf
dinner	spaghetti
dessert	black cherry jello
drink	fruit punch
kind of store	electronics store
dream vacation place	Florida
month	September
pet	Shih tzu dog
animal to be	bat
secret power to have	to throw out lightning bolts

David Jiminez, age 9

adventure	"falling off my loft"
wish	to be able to skateboard
job to have	video game programmer
president	Lincoln
thing to do on Saturday	watch television and play basketball

Cavana Lee-Hampel, age 12

color	aquamarine
song	"Straighten Up and Fly Right"
instrument	piano
way to travel	boat
amusement ride	bumper cars
hiding place	in a tree
monster	brontosaurus
toy	Pinocchio doll
treasure	necklace
indoor game	I doubt it
outdoor game	treasure hunts
thing to wear	patchwork sweater
thing to make	drawings of cats
thing to collect	snail shells and nature objects
time of day	dawn
picture book	*Make Way for Ducklings*
chapter book	*Island of the Blue Dolphins*
author	Norton Juster
movie	*Raiders of the Lost Ark*
fairy tale character	Rumpelstiltskin
dinner	"my Mama's spaghetti casserole"
dessert	pumpkin pie
drink	piña colada
dream vacation place	West Germany
month	February
animal to be	fish
pet	sheepdog
secret power to have	"to blink myself anywhere"
adventure	being trapped in an elevator

Fig. 4—*Continued*

Cavana Lee-Hampel, age 12

wish	to end racism, jealousy, and greed
job to have	dancer
president	Kennedy
thing to do on Saturday	go horseback riding

Because these interviews tap into children's interests and pleasures in a non-threatening way, they can help an adult discern what matters most to them. They can give a sense of students' home lives, allowing teachers to see them in other contexts. Questions about what animal a child would like to be, or what secret power he or she would like to possess enable a child to indirectly express personal fantasies.

What can one actually deduce about these four children and their interests that could help in finding them the right book? Which of them might enjoy a wild ride in Mr. Toad's automobile? Who might enjoy a walk with a hobbit? Who might be moved by hearing Paula Fox's *One-Eyed Cat?* Who might be searching for an information book about computers? Who might be drawn to a biography of Martha Graham or Isadora Duncan?

What could one speculate about these children as individuals, with unique learning characteristics? Which of them might be challenged by an art project? Who might enjoy working independently? Who might prefer working with a partner or a group? Who might learn best through a hands-on experience? Who might be a dreamer? Who might have trouble sitting still?

Four Profiles

Eight-year-old Marcus is an eager learner, bright, knowledgeable, highly motivated. He soaks up information and is always listening hard. In group discussions he can be chatty and rambunctious, often blurting things out. Teachers may have to "sit" on him, but they never want to curtail his enthusiasm. He has a clever wit and loves to banter. He sees the humor in a situation. Marcus is at the stage where he enjoys reading adventure books such as Peggy Parish's *Key to the Treasure*. A generous and caring boy, he fully enjoys his comradeship with others. He seems on the threshold of becoming a leader, and one can count on his strengths to spark special library events. He was a catalyst in one special science project, organizing and leading a group of kids to the park for plant specimens.

Elvira, another eight-year-old, is a keen, vibrant, and gregarious child. An avid reader, she enjoys both realistic fiction and fantasy books. She was captivated by the Ramona series and by *The Indian in the Cupboard* (Banks). She is purposeful in her work and takes school seriously. She enjoys writing, researching, and thinking things out. Her projects are based on sound ideas and usually have a depth to them. She is flexible and works well in all types of situations. In the social context, she gravitates toward small groups of girls and can be involved in intense friendships. She contributes her artistic skills to library celebrations by creating drawings, posters, and props.

David is a gentle, poetic, reserved nine-year-old with a deep, infectious laugh. He possesses a strong sense of integrity. Other students can count on him as a good and loyal friend. He has great powers of concentration, and can become fully immersed in a book or a film. He has a passion for fantasy works such as the *Lord of the Rings* trilogy. Although he can be cautious in new situations, David has flourished in the library thematic exploring program. He has expressed his humorous and spontaneous self in a variety of roles, performing as a Greek god, a magician, the Big Bad Wolf, and as boisterous Ned Land at Captain Nemo's trial.

Cavana is an eleven-year-old artist, individualistic and introspective. She loves creative risk-taking and moves freely from one medium to the next, especially enjoying dance and mime. Her choice of dawn as her favorite time of day reveals her private, contemplative nature. It is easy to see why she was so responsive to *The Island of the Blue Dolphins* (O'Dell). As she enters adolescence she is becoming more tuned in to her peers and their needs, and is more willing to compromise in collaborative efforts. Her grace, freedom of movement, and strong inner delight were evident when she performed in an African folktale during one of the library celebrations.

Getting a fix on the needs and characteristics of students as individuals requires a good deal of informal interaction—talking and listening to children, and being aware of the issues they are facing. Insights into all kinds of behavior can help in obtaining the fullest sense of a child. They can help identify children who lack self-esteem, to detect patterns of isolation. Certain children may struggle in the library media center and do better in homerooms because of their difficulty in separating. If the library media specialist is sensitive to the concerns and worries of children, he or she can help them to identify and express their feelings and elaborate on them. The specialist can help them delve into their imaginations and be more in touch with their fantasies and dreams.

The Impact of Rapid Social Change on Development

Today, students of all ages are struggling with problems that are special to children growing up in the last decade of the twentieth century. These problems, which often arise from changes in family structure and in the economy, can sometimes interfere with learning and development. Many young people must deal with a chaotic day-to-day existence in which adults may be absent, neglectful, or downright threatening. Latchkey children, for instance, may experience loneliness and have an intense need to release and communicate. Interracial and minority children may have to cope with both subtle and overt forms of racism.

Too many children have to deal with scenarios of poverty, hunger, and abuse. Some children may be overwhelmed by living with two families and adapting to two different lifestyles. Urban and suburban children may struggle to feel centered as they attend three after-school programs in the course of one week. Older children are forced to respond to peer pressures, academic pressures, and pressures to experiment with alcohol and drugs. Most educators agree that children of all ages "today are more exposed to the cares and worries, to the life and ways of adults than ever before, largely through mass media. Adults, themselves confronted with feelings of helplessness over issues such as nuclear arms control, the pollution of our air, soil, and waters, are perhaps less reassuring than they used to be."[10]

Herbert Zimilies echoes this concern in his study of adult perceptions of the changing American child. Educators and other professionals report that children seem to reach developmental landmarks at an earlier age. Traditional concepts of age-appropriate behavior are changing; parents and teachers feel they have less advice to give, less knowledge to impart. Middle-class children are portrayed as extremely single-minded. These are children with strong material concerns, whose heroes, if any, are the big moneymakers, the rock stars and athletes. Many of them seem to feel removed from moral issues and may not view cheating or lying in such a negative light. "Children are more practical and goal-directed. They seem to be genuinely confused about what is right and wrong except in so far as it has implications for goal achievement."[11]

Although these judgments are hard to accept, the problems they describe must be acknowledged if educators are to plan meaningful school programs for students. If the library media center is to become a significant place in children's lives, then the library media specialist has to take into account all of their struggles. He or she must wonder about their world outside of the school, and must assess their conversations and narratives for clues to their wishes and dreams, to their interests and passions, to their sorrows and confusion.

This knowledge can guide the library media specialist in establishing an environment that is stimulating and aesthetically pleasing, a place where children feel comfortable and expansive, whatever the purpose of their visit—a class session, delivering a note from the teacher, returning a piece of equipment, beginning a research project, or looking for a book that "isn't boring." The library media center should be a place where children can find a private space for reading and daydreaming, or where they can work or talk quietly with a friend. It should be a place in which sessions are structured so there are clear rituals and where there is a sense of closure and children coming back together.

The exploring of powerful themes in such a safe, trusting environment can help young people to feel hopeful and at ease, to sort matters out, to begin to articulate their concerns and define themselves. It can help them to develop strengths and to tap inner resources. It can also help adults take stock of their own important contributions to students' lives and learning. The library media center can become a kind of retreat within the school, and a caring library media specialist can provide a significant measure of the stability and continuity that school has come to provide for children of all ages.

Notes

1. John Dewey, "My Pedagogic Creed," in *John Dewey on Education: Selected Writings,* ed. Reginald D. Archambault (New York: Modern Library, 1964), p. 428.

2. Howard Gardner's *Frames of Mind: A Theory of Multiple Intelligences* (New York: Basic Books, 1983) is summarized by Marge Scherer in "How Many Ways Is a Child Intelligent?" *Instructor* 94:32–35 (January, 1985).

3. For a summary and bibliography on this topic, see Rita Dunn, Jeffrey S. Beaudry, and Angela Klavas, "Survey of Research on Learning Styles," *Educational Leadership* 46:50–57 (March, 1989).

4. Of numerous critiques of large and impersonal school environments, see the report issued by the Carnegie Foundation for the Advancement of Teaching, *An Imperiled Generation: Saving Urban Schools* (Princeton, N.J.: Princeton Univ. Pr., 1988). Theodore R. Sizer's Coalition of Essential Schools also stresses the importance of the personalization of teaching and learning; *see* his "Afterward: An Experiment for Horace," in *Horace's Compromise* (Boston, Mass.: Houghton Mifflin, 1985), pp. 222–37.

5. Erik H. Erikson, *Childhood and Society,* 35th anniv. ed. (New York: W. W. Norton, 1986).

6. A good summary of the extensive writings of Jean Piaget may be found in *A Piaget Primer: How a Child Thinks,* by Dorothy G. Singer and Tracey A. Revenson (New York: New American Library, 1978).

7. Developmental models are summarized in "Understanding Children," from the 7th edition of Zena Sutherland and May Hill Arbuthnot, *Children and Books* (Glenview, Ill.: Scott, Foresman & Co., 1986), pp. 20–40. Book reviews in the *Bulletin of the Chicago Center for Children's Books* include subjects with a developmental focus. See also Sharon S. Dreyer's series, *The Bookfinder: A Guide to Children's Literature about the Needs and Problems of Youth Aged 2–15,* vols. 1–4 (Circle Pines, Minn.: American Guidance Service, 1977–89). Developmental stages are also prominent in reader response theory.

8. Jamaica Kincaid, *Annie John* (New York: New American Library, 1983), p. 85.

9. Dorothy Watson and Paul Crowley suggest a number of informal activities that can help teachers gather information about students. See "How Can We Implement a Whole Language Approach?" in Constance Weaver, *Reading Process and Practice: From Socio-Psycholinguistics to Whole Language* (Portsmouth, N.H.: Heinemann, 1988), pp. 235–41.

10. Joan Cenedella, "Progressivism and Social Studies: Principles and Problems," unpublished paper presented October 18, 1986, at Teachers College, Columbia University, New York City, p. 8.

11. Herbert Zimiles, "The Changing American Child: The Perspective of Educators." A Report to the National Commission on Excellence in Education (New York: Bank Street College of Education, October 1982), p. 38. *See also* articles by Alex Molnar, William Ayers, Marian Wright Edelman, and others, in the section "Contemporary Issues: Children" in *Educational Leadership* 46:68–81 (May, 1989).

References

Books

Banks, Lynne R. *The Indian in the Cupboard.* Doubleday, 1985.

Burningham, John. *Mr. Gumpy's Outing.* Holt, 1971.

Byars, Betsy. *The Eighteenth Emergency.* Viking, 1973.

Dahl, Roald. *Danny: The Champion of the World.* Knopf, 1975.

Fenner, Carol. *Tigers in the Cellar.* Harcourt, 1973.

Fox, Paula. *One-Eyed Cat.* Bradbury, 1984.

Frank, Anne. *Anne Frank: The Diary of a Young Girl.* Doubleday, 1967.

Holling, Holling C. *Paddle-to-the-Sea.* Houghton, 1980.

Holm, Anne. *North to Freedom.* Harcourt, 1965.

Kincaid, Jamaica. *Annie John.* Farrar, 1985.

Konigsburg, E. L. *Jennifer, Hecate, MacBeth, William McKinley, and Me, Elizabeth.* Atheneum, 1967.

Krauss, Ruth. *The Carrot Seed,* ill. by Crockett Johnson. Harper, 1945.

Krumgold, Joseph. *. . . and now Miguel.* Crowell, 1953.

O'Dell, Scott. *Island of the Blue Dolphin.* Houghton, 1960.

Parish, Peggy. *Key to the Treasure.* Dell, 1980.

Paterson, Katherine. *Bridge to Terabithia.* Crowell, 1977.

Russo, Marisabina. *The Line Up Book.* Greenwillow, 1986.

Scheer, Julian. *Rain Makes Applesauce.* Holiday, 1964.

Slepian, Jan. *The Alfred Summer.* Macmillan, 1980.

Speare, Elizabeth. *The Witch of Blackbird Pond.* Houghton, 1958.

Steig, William. *Sylvester and the Magic Pebble.* Simon, 1969.

Stolz, Mary. *The Noonday Friends.* Harper, 1965.

White, E. B. *Charlotte's Web.* Harper, 1952.

Films and Videos

J.T. CBS Television, 1969. 51 min.

My Life as a Dog, dir. by Lasse Hallstrom. Sweden, 1985. 100 min.

The World of Henry Orient, dir. by George Roy Hill. United Artists, 1964. 115 min.

Literature and Literacy Perspectives

Literature-Based Language Arts

The process of thematic exploring through literature is based on assumptions and techniques described in the wealth of books and articles on literature-based language arts, whole language approaches, and on the writing process.[1] This approach links many ways of learning and communicating, as well as many areas of content. In this type of curriculum, an integrated language arts framework of reading, writing, speaking, and listening meshes with other content areas—social studies, science, music, art, and drama. Sufficient time is set aside for literacy activities conducted in flexible groupings: independent reading of self-chosen texts, listening as a group to stories read aloud by others, book sharing among peers, shared and independent writing activities, dramatizations, and other types of story presentation. Children are actively playing with ideas and experimenting with words to communicate the ideas.

Teachers draw upon a variety of resources and flexible instructional approaches that are familiar to library media specialists, whose programs and collections should reflect a commitment to children having literary, film, and artistic encounters as a vital part of their core curriculum.

> The school library media program includes the sharing of ideas and stories through storytelling, slide and video productions, and dramatic presentations. Students of all ages use modern video equipment and simple cameras to create visual images to convey information and to communicate with others. Students teach each other and confer with the teacher or library media specialist as they work in the center on such learning projects. Teachers, the school library media specialist, and students encourage each other to explore new materials and try out different sources of information.[2]

Thematic exploring in the library media center supports and extends the literature-based language arts program in many ways. Students' motivation and skills development are increased in reading, writing, speaking, and listening. Students are helped to examine literature through individual and group explorations. They develop new understandings about literary genres, story elements, styles, and voices. They begin to apply criteria for evaluating works in discussions and in written criticisms. They learn how to draw upon the ideas of others as inspiration for shaping their own personal visions. Children learn how to share their personal responses to works with others, and to use them as springboards for creating original works. They become consciously aware of the aesthetic dimensions of literature.

Many activities emphasize reading and interpreting written words, abstracting information, and making practical connections. Students read from a variety of sources in this process. There are no basal readers or worksheets. Individuals can pursue different aspects of a theme. For example, an exploration of "flight" could lead one child to a picture book such as *Gorky Rises* (Steig) or to a folktale such as *The Fool of the World and the Flying Ship* (Ransome). Another child might be drawn to a fantasy novel such as *The Wonderful Flight to the Mushroom Planet* (Cameron) or a play such as *Peter Pan* (Barrie). Still another might prefer a nonfiction book on hang gliding, or a biography of Amelia Earhart.

Written Responses to Literature

Thematic exploring encourages children to discover new authors, to appreciate and be aware of their various styles and voices, and to use their works as models to further their own creative writing and literary criticism. Thematic explorations can move children to look at the different literary genres. They might look at the way different authors begin their stories, and create their own beginnings of mysteries, fantasies, or realistic stories about kids like themselves. Then they examine whole works, looking at characters, style, plot structure, and mood. They may write reviews or personal reactions. Finally, they may use the books as springboards for original stories, plays, and other creative activities initiated either by them or by their teachers. This can be the end of the unit, or it can grow into a full-fledged journey and celebration. It all depends.

Take, for example, a typical genre study, in which students identified some distinctive literary devices, assessed their effectiveness, and used the best samples as models for their own literary efforts. Sixth graders began a library unit on mysteries by looking closely at beginnings—the ways authors create atmosphere and set up successful story lines.

Natalie Babbit introduces a mysterious element at the beginning of *Goody Hall:*

> The blacksmith stood in the door of his shop and sniffed the May breeze hopefully. "There's something in the air, no doubt about it," he said to himself with satisfaction. "Something is going to happen."[3]

Blair's Nightmare (Snyder) effectively uses the device of a dream to set up the anxieties of the main character:

> David had been dreaming that he was in the school cafeteria, and for a moment the noise fitted right in. In the dream he was carrying an enormous slippery tray full of food and looking for a place to sit down, but all the seats were filled—except one. The one vacant chair was at a table where a bunch of guys stared at him and said things like, "Get lost," and "This seat is saved."[4]

Ellen Raskin injects lightness and humor into the opening of *The Westing Game:*

> The sun sets in the west (just about everyone knows that), but Sunset Towers faced east. Strange! Sunset Towers faced east and had no towers. This glittery, glassy apartment house stood alone on the Lake Michigan shore five stories high. Five empty stories high. Then one day (it happened to be the Fourth of July), a most uncommon-looking delivery boy rode around town slipping letters under the doors of the chosen tenants-to-be. The letters were signed Barney Northrup. The delivery boy was sixty-two years old, and there was no such person as Barney Northrup.[5]

Looking carefully at beginnings like these helped children see how they might pique curiosity and pull a reader into the action. They tried to use words crisply, vibrantly, and economically as they created their own beginnings of mysteries. They discussed undercurrents and subtexts. They recalled those times of feeling at ease and relaxed, and then having the mood change abruptly. As a starting point students could choose a sound (ping, clang, tick, hiss, hum, scratch), an object (whistle, shell, toy soldier, compass, charm, chess piece), or a person (peddler, kitemaker, pretzel vendor, street mime, bird watcher, inventor). They could also make up a title or use one of the following titles: *Did They Ever Return?; The Double; The Ghost of Columbus Avenue; Last Words; No Trespassing; Only a Worm; The People Who Lived Below; The Six-Foot Gerbil; A Slight Ache.* Here are some samples of their mystery beginnings.

> *The Chess Piece.* One day after coming home from school, I walked into my room and heard somebody grunt "checkmate." At first I thought it was my little sister but she doesn't know how to play chess too well and she had no one to play with. (Remy Chait, age 12)

> *Key to Nowhere.* Spike and Chip were looking around in their grandfather's attic. (There wasn't anything else to do on that dreary day in April.) While they were up there, they found pirate costumes, old Dutch costumes, and a medium-sized chest. The chest was very old and it hadn't started to decay yet. They were anxious to find out what was in there, but the lock was rusted shut and they had no way to open it. (Brian Williams, age 12)

The Double. Richard and his two snotty twin sisters sat in a limo, talking about their father's will. They all had a picture in their minds of the 750 millions they would inherit when he dies, and they all had a twitch in their eyes. (Lucius Hill, age 12)

After analyzing a genre in some depth, and trying to apply the conventions they have discovered to their own writing, students are often ready to take on the role of literary critic. The library media specialist can help them frame questions to develop criteria for evaluating picture books and novels. Do the illustrations enhance the story? Do stereotypes prevail? What is the quality of the writing? Does the author create a vivid sense of place? Do the characters have depth or do they seem superficial? Does the ending seem plausible? Here are some fifth graders' written responses to certain books. Note the different meanings Kate and Ethan attach to the idea of getting "lost" in a book.

The Dream Stealer (Maguire) was very descriptive. It was funny, and you didn't get lost. You always knew what was happening. The plot was excellent and the characters could charm anyone. (Kate Schaaf, age 11)

I liked *The Dream Stealer* because I could get lost in it. It was exciting and had the right funny touches. I really liked the idea of just a wolf haunting all of Russia. (Ethan Nichtern, age 11)

The Story of King Arthur (Pyle) was an absolutely wonderful book! It was strong, it was moving. It had courage, sadness, even a little romance. I could never put it down. (Sarah Tucker, age 11)

Through the exploration of literary genres, the library becomes a "place where students are saturated with stories, seeing them, hearing them, talking about them, reading about them, writing about them."[6]

Authors as Models

The reading aloud of Seymour Reit's *Benvenuto* by the teacher of eight- and nine-year-olds led to an exploration of dragons that also involved the library program. Encouraged by the teacher and library media specialist, children, in the spirit of kind-hearted Benvenuto, created their own dragon books. A series of "round table" discussions helped them to think about developing a strong character, an intriguing plot, and a descriptive sense of place. Everyone in the class worked on at least three drafts before illustrating the final version of a story. Students with different interests and abilities were deeply engaged, and each was able to find his or her own voice as an author. For example, nine-year-old Sylvia Gale has become a meticulous wordsmith. An enthusiastic reader who appreciates beautiful language, she opens her story, "The Dragon of Catalma Castle," with this introduction.

No-Name was a handsome dragon with scales and a medium-sized tail at the end of his small body. Now I will tell you about Catalma Castle. The castle had been used by royal kings and queens back in the days of King Arthur, but now it was deserted and run down, and when visitors came, it was very rare.

In contrast to the fairy tale setting and literary quality of Sylvia's language, Asa Scott's writing style is gritty and direct. In his "The Break Dance Dragon," a baby dragon is "afraid to spit fire because of a vision." It seems that when he was young "a big blast of fire came out of his mouth and set fire to his crib." And now he keeps dwelling on this incident. Asa's story, set in the real world of an urban neighborhood, draws on his own early childhood fears and represents a real breakthrough for him. This was one of the first times he wrote with such dedication and pleasure.

The dragon study culminated with a visit from the author, Seymour Reit. He and the class of young authors discussed the writing process and what happened when they felt frustrated. Mr. Reit explained the way he incorporated various real neighborhood locales into his story setting. The children then shared their dragon books and feasted on homemade dragon cookies. One could see that the author was moved that his book had so sparked their imaginations and energies. It seemed that all concerned—adults and children—had connected with their minds and hearts, that they had come together as both readers and storymakers. "If we want children to learn and take delight in reading, we need to make environments rich in literacy events where there is a reason for reading, where they see a reason for reading, and find personal meaning in stories."[7]

Oral Responses to Literature

Thematic exploring encourages students to listen to stories aesthetically, simply enjoying their rhythms and sounds. They may listen to a variety of folktales and discern the values being transmitted. Students also share their own original narratives and, as storytellers, experience the delight of truly engaging their listeners. They learn that all the stories have not yet been written, and that stories belong to everyone and not just the teacher or library media specialist. They can personally appreciate the gift Anansi makes in *A Story, A Story* (Haley) when, after obtaining the Sky God's box of stories, he opens it up and the stories fly "to all the corners of the earth, including this one."[8]

Storytelling can become a springboard for other kinds of oral activity involving music and drama. Dramatic improvisation motivates students to draw upon inner resources to create a character, a world. It requires a high degree of empathy and insight into cause and effect. It can reveal what they have understood about a story and how a story has affected them. Terry Salinger explores the value of providing such experiences:

This movement from oneself to a new character takes place when roles are assigned and parts are learned or when children are asked to improvise a person or animal. They strengthen their abilities to present ideas orally, improve their enunciation, and develop poise and self-confidence. In improvising characters, children experience focused role-playing and often can release emotion, express humor, and gain insight into conflicts or distressing situations by trying different roles and appropriate voices, movements, and characteristics.[9]

Thematic exploring offers many opportunities for such character development. In the creation of past worlds like the "Wild West" or "Renaissance," children search for information about the kinds of individuals who lived and worked in these times. Each person creates a character, developing his or her personality through the writing of a character sketch or monologue. These may include a character's habits and quirks. Here is a sample of tall tales conceived for a Wild West unit.

I'm Bisquick Betty. I'm what people call the Julia Child of the West. I can flip a flapjack faster than you can say "hot diggity dog." I can make cactus bread and rattlesnake stew. (Zoey Johnson, age 11)

My name is Dr. Sagebrush and I can cure any illness. I was born in a pill bottle, and if you believe that, I will cure you of arthritis. I have even cured a man who said he was the President. I gave him a tonic of beeswax and the insides of a crow. One woman was complaining of headaches, and I gave her my famous tonic of grass green water. Yes, that's right . . . grass green water. I got 20 dollars, too! (Asha Logan, age 10)

I'm Tall Tale Tim. I'm the best storyteller in the West. I tell stories about the one-mile-high giants, the table that talks, and the monster who ate Dallas. The strange thing is that nobody believes me. Look at my face. Can't you trust me? When I was a kid my textbook ate my school work. My favorite tale is about when I caught the mile-long fish in the one-half-mile river. (Timothy Gillam, age 11)

When children at last animate their characters in some form of dramatic play, they have already lived with the character for a time. They have developed a sense of what motivates the character and of what this person's fears and pleasures are. This makes the performing more sensitive and thoughtful, and more authentic. This evolving of a character demands the constant use and interplay of the reading, writing, speaking, and listening processes.

Oral responses to literature can take many other forms. After listening to *Ty's One-Man Band* (Walter), a group of first and second graders formed their own jug band, enthusiastically playing the bottles, combs and spoons. After enjoying *That Man Is Talking to His Toes* (Hann), another group amused themselves playing the telephone game. That book thereafter always elicited some chuckling, for it was associated with word play, nonsense, and a positive group experience. An eight-year-old, having slurped his lemon as Old Sneep in a dramatization of *Lentil* (McClosky), will likely feel a part of that book forever.

Building an Interpretive Community

Thematic exploring requires an interactive stance that is strongly aesthetic and personal; children must integrate the cognitive and affective dimensions of learning for the journey to succeed. In explorations where they can reveal their feelings about the beauty and emotional impact of a work, students begin to develop a personal framework for aesthetic inquiry. Through repeated encounters with works and with the responses of others to these works, children begin to work together in what Vandergrift describes as an interpretive community whose collective understandings about literature are based on shared individual responses to stories.[10]

Yet one of the greatest challenges for teachers today, regardless of age or stage, is motivating children to read—finding the right book for the right child at the right time. Even pleasure reading requires commitment and engagement. So much in children's environments leads them away from reading. Television has accustomed them to being bombarded with stimuli. They learn to be passive, to tune out. Although there is conflicting research on the effects of television on children's learning, teachers report that the fragmented, staccato format of presenting information has had adverse effects on students' attention span. Children attempting to read their first long chapter book may struggle as much with the demand for sustained attention time as with comprehending more complex plots or more challenging vocabulary. ("This is boring!" "I can't read it.") Reading may not be an important activity in the home environment. Family members may not choose to read, may have limited time to read, or may not have developed adequate skills.

Partnerships among classroom teachers, library media specialists, and reading or language arts specialists can be very effective in countering negative environmental influences. As a team, educators can better monitor the progress of individual children, providing guidance and support to ensure their success both as readers and writers. Such instructional partnerships are vital ingredients in the development of successful thematic exploring units. In this context, Weaver and other whole-language advocates would describe thematic exploring as part of a student-centered curriculum in which "teachers find out about students' interests, abilities, and needs, and then use that information in curriculum planning and in instructional procedures."[11]

Part 2 of this book introduces the reader to a number of specific themes, ideas, and activities that evolved through such partnerships, and can be adapted to almost any curriculum content or student population. At its best, thematic exploring becomes a collaborative quest for meaning that brings students and teachers together not only as a "community of readers," but of talkers and listeners as well.[12] The following chapters offer the library media specialist some special ways of contributing to such a community, functioning as a guide to adventures with language, not only in the library, but throughout the school.

Notes

1. *See* Eleanor Kulleseid and Dorothy Strickland, *Literature, Literacy, and Learning* (Chicago: American Library Assn., 1989) for a concise summary of theory and practice.

2. American Assn. of School Librarians and Assn. for Educational Communications and Technology, *Information Power: Guidelines for School Library Media Programs* (Chicago: American Library Assn.; Washington, D.C.: Assn. for Educational Communications and Technology, 1988), p. 17.

3. Natalie Babbitt, *Goody Hall* (New York: Farrar, Straus & Giroux, 1971), p. 3.

4. Zilpha Keatley Snyder, *Blair's Nightmare* (New York: Atheneum, 1984), p. 3.

5. Ellen Raskin, *The Westing Game* (New York: Dutton, 1978), p. 1.

6. David M. Brown, "A Half-Time Compromise to the Whole Language Approach," in *School Library Media Annual 1988 Volume Six,* ed. Jane Bandy Smith (Englewood, Colo.: Libraries Unlimited, 1988), p. 41.

7. Charlotte S. Huck et al., *Children's Literature in the Elementary School,* 4th ed. (New York: Holt, Rinehart and Winston, 1987), p. 30.

8. Gail E. Haley, *A Story, A Story* (New York: Atheneum, 1970), unpaged; final page.

9. Terry S. Salinger, *Language Arts and Literacy for Young Children* (Columbus, Ohio: Merrill, 1988), p. 45.

10. Kay E. Vandergrift, "Using Reader-Response Theory to Influence Collection Development and Program Planning for Children," in *Information Seeking: Basing Services on Users' Behaviors,* ed. Jana Varlejs (Jefferson, Md.: McFarland, 1987), pp. 52–66.

11. Dorothy Watson and Paul Crowley, "How Can We Implement a Whole-Language Approach?" in Constance Weaver, *Reading Process and Practice: From Socio-Psycholinguistics to Whole Language* (Portsmouth, N.H.: Heinemann, 1988), p. 235ff.

12. Susan Hepler, as quoted in "Developing Readers," by Charlotte S. Huck and Kristen Jeffers Kerstetter, in *Children's Literature in the Reading Program,* ed. Bernice E. Cullinan (Newark Del.: International Reading Assn., 1987), p. 37.

References

Babbit, Natalie. *Goody Hall*. Farrar, 1971.

Barrie, J. M. *Peter Pan*. Scribner's, 1950.

Cameron, Eleanor. *The Wonderful Flight to the Mushroom Planet*. Little, 1954.

Haley, Gail E. *A Story, A Story*. Macmillan, 1970.

Hann, Jacquie. *That Man Is Talking to His Toes*. Four Winds, 1976.

McCloskey, Robert. *Lentil*. Viking, 1940.

Maguire, Gregory. *The Dream Stealer*. Harper, 1983.

Pyle, Howard. *The Story of King Arthur and His Knights*. Scribner's, 1933.

Ransome, Arthur. *The Fool of the World and the Flying Ship,* ill. by Uri Shulevitz. Farrar, 1968.
Raskin, Ellen. *The Westing Game.* Dutton, 1978.
Reit, Seymour. *Benvenuto.* Addison-Wesley, 1974.
Snyder, Zilpha K. *Blair's Nightmare.* Atheneum, 1984.
Steig, William. *Gorky Rises.* Farrar, 1980.
Walter, Mildred Pitts. *Ty's One-Man Band,* ill. by Margot Tomes. Four Winds, 1980.

PART 2

An Explorer's Guide to Five Journeys

The next five chapters are devoted to the exploration of universal themes that can engage adults and children on cognitive, emotional, social, and aesthetic levels, themes that can be readily woven into traditional content areas of the curriculum. Each chapter is divided into three main sections: "Introduction to the Theme," "Routes," and a "Journey Log."

"Introduction to the Theme" is a springboard for the study, providing the substance, the contextual map. Issues are identified, questions are raised, and literary works are suggested to illuminate the content. The library media specialist can use this section to consider broadly the various dimensions of a theme, or to zero in on a particular aspect or detail.

"Routes" offers alternative ways of taking a journey. The library media specialist decides what might be useful or relevant for the program, for a particular group of students, for a given time of year. The journey may take place over many sessions; it may be a single outing. Whatever the educational goal or program emphasis, "Routes" is intended to be used flexibly, as a menu of specific activites from which library media specialists may pick and choose for planning beginnings, excursions, and/or celebrations.

"Routes" first suggests ideas for beginning the journey with younger (Pre-K–Grade 2), middle (Grades 3–5), and older (Grades 6-up) students. The point of entry should spur students toward further exploration and excite both curiosity and imagination. The activities suggested are just possibilities. Some are simple to prepare and can be done in one session. Others are more complex and elaborate; they may require two or three sessions.

Excursions enable children to explore a number of ideas that excite their curiosity, and to move toward activities that are appropriate for their ages and interests. Excursions are grouped into four categories: verbal; written; art and music; and research. Verbal excursions emphasize activities and projects that allow children to develop as storytellers, actors, speakers, and listeners. Written excursions focus on helping children develop fluidity, clarity, and a sense of style in the creation of stories, poems, plays, and expository forms. Art and music excursions encourage students to cultivate an aesthetic sense, including appreciation of imagery and mood. Research excursions stimulate students to be playfully involved in quests for information that require use of a diversity of sources.

Celebrations are culminating experiences intended to bring a thematic exploration to a satisfying and triumphant conclusion. Sometimes the idea for a celebration comes early in a study, and helps to shape the course of the journey. More often, the idea evolves during the journey itself. Celebrations provide a sense of festivity and fellowship and may involve community members transforming the library media center into some kind of imaginary world. Celebrations integrate the different threads of the journey and allow children to share their learnings and creations.

The third and final section of each chapter is devoted to a "Journey Log." The log is the author's personal account of a real journey, a case study of a specific curriculum unit that has grown out of one school's group life. Each journey described follows the thematic exploring framework from the conceptual stage (choosing the theme) through the culminating project (celebrating the journey). Unlike the open-ended menu approach of "Routes," the "Journey Log" presents a sequence of interrelated activities that have a cumulative effect. The section concludes with an evaluation of the learning outcomes produced by the curriculum unit. "Journey Logs" are intended to have transfer value. Library media specialists can use the narratives as models for shaping new journeys that reflect their own special strengths, concerns, and knowledge of the school community.

Essentials for a Successful Journey

Vision and personal investment are vital for a successful journey. Library media specialists must make the journeys their own. They may choose to experiment with a small scale adventure, and initially they may face resistance and experience some lonely moments. They will need to persevere until others sense what is happening, and begin to value and use the power of the journey format. Whatever the circumstances, library media specialists will have to deal with three variables: partnerships, time schedules, and material resources.

Partnerships are essential. Obviously, this is a collaborative process and the support of others is crucial. An enormous amount of detail work is involved. Activities include planning sessions, organizing and collecting materials, writing scripts, creating costumes and props, and rehearsing. Brainstorming and exchanging ideas with others is also exciting. Cooperative planning inspires almost everyone to give extra time and effort. The library media specialist and teacher must work out a division of labor and establish common educational goals. In the first year the library media specialist might choose to focus on only one theme with a particularly responsive teacher and class. Other possible recruits might include older children as library assistants, parent volunteers, senior volunteers, and college interns.

Flexible time schedules are essential; they are the building blocks for each adventure. The library media specialist will need to develop strategies for working sometimes with small groups, sometimes with half groups or even individuals. On occasion, extended periods of time may be needed to work with a group for an entire morning or afternoon, even a full day. This more expansive time frame is especially vital if a celebration or field study project is involved. The library media specialist may need to convey that thematic exploring does not take away from skill sessions or literature sharing but, instead, incorporates these activities in a more dynamic and personal manner.

Material resources are also important, but less crucial to the success of the project. The library media specialist may need to inform others that thematic exploring does not depend on an elaborate supply of materials; it can be financed on a shoestring. In fact, such programs lend themselves to scavenging, improvising, using what is available, and making contacts with the larger community.

The First Journey:
Villains and Bullies

Introduction to the Theme

When a bully is operating, children are always at risk. Their sense of belonging and sense of place become threatened. A bully's unpredictable behavior can trigger a child's insecurities. "Where do I fit in? What happens if the group turns against me? What if I'm the one who is scapegoated?" Villains and bullies represent to children the fear of losing control and being annihilated. To be oppressed by a bully is to feel incompetent and powerless, and this can diminish a child's sense of worth.

Villains

Everywhere in the landscape of literature, villains are operating and scheming. They inhabit myths (Loki), folktales (Babi Yaga), fairy tales (the Giant), fantasy books (the Queen of Hearts), legends (the Sheriff of Nottingham), and mysteries (Moriarity). Classical villains are universal, living in all times and places. They may be diabolical and resilient, but, because they are larger than life, children can feel safe and enjoy them from a distance. Children can hiss the landlord in a melodrama and know justice will prevail. Such villains can be colorful and dramatic, and they cannot hurt you. Sometimes children even feel an affection for them. Through wearing masks and costumes or simply role playing, children can feel a measure of control over what may have once seemed scary. They can howl in the woods, cackle over a brew, and walk in the footsteps of the giant.

The most compelling villains have a complexity, a vulnerable part. They are more intelligent, more textured, more stylish. Darth Vader from *Star Wars* (Lucas), for example, has had an enormous impact on children's imaginations. He has strength and presence, vigorous movement, and a booming, resonant voice. Viewers sense that this character knows who he is. They can understand his anger.

Shakespearean characters like Othello and Iago also possess this kind of power and dimension.

The role of the villain in literature and film is to obstruct, to provide conflict, tension, imposing barriers. A pleasure for children is anticipating the comeuppance. How will the villain get it in the end? Will there be revenge or poetic justice? It can be exciting to develop criteria for defining a villain. Who qualifies? How is a particular character evil or destructive? Is the character's intention actually to hurt someone? Is the character truly a villain or more of a rogue or scoundrel? Do his or her actions seem credible in relation to his or her history?

Other discussions may center on provocative questions about specific stereotypes of evil. Why is it hard to think of many women villains, other than witches? And are all witches practitioners of evil? Why do the good guys wear white and the bad guys wear black? What does this mean for minority children? Why do snakes and wolves play sinister roles in so many folktales? How could a person be considered a villain by some people and a hero by others? How does villainy become institutionalized and the practices of bullies legally sanctioned?

Bullies

Bullies are much closer to home. They exist, not in the safety of Long Ago, but in everyday life. Children may encounter them in the family, the neighborhood, the school. The bullies don't always get it in the end, and there might not seem to be anyone around to ease the situation.

How do bullies intimidate? What are their tactics? Why do they seem unrelenting? How do they make others uncomfortable? Do they always look for someone's weaknesses? How do they sustain their power or grip? How do they attract their followers? How do children cope with bullies? What can they do about them?

A first encounter with a bully can be devastating. It can trigger feelings of fear, anxiety, embarrassment, confusion, anger, and powerlessness. "Why am I being picked on?" It can distort a child's self-image and shake his or her confidence. Just being able to explore what motivates a bully can have a releasing effect on children. They begin to understand a bully's posturing and aggressiveness, a bully's irrational behavior and psychological makeup. The idea that they can take action, that they have some options, can be very empowering.

Students need to be exposed to both personal accounts and fictional works in which the bully is understood and defeated. They need to be aware of solutions that might work. The bully gets smaller as children learn others have had similar experiences. These kinds of discussions expose the bully. The library media specialist might want to relate a childhood story to give students perspective. "See, these things pass. The nightmare will end. This bad period won't last forever."

Children also need to see that all people can be bullies at times—when they pick on younger siblings, or take advantage of those who are physically weaker. But when they play the bully, others are going to react, and there will be consequences. When they tease with an edge, someone could get hurt, and the teaser is accountable. This is a powerful theme. The exploration may involve younger children simply identifying negative behavior. ("The wolf shouldn't have tricked her.") It may involve older students examining issues of child abuse. It is a theme that touches everyone, and exploring it could give children insight and hope.

> In the book, *All Quiet on the Western Front* (Remarque), the officer who Paul had in basic training was a bully. I forgot his name but it began with a "K." Anyway, his main reason for being a bully was probably in civilian life, he had a job where he was not in charge of a lot of people. When he got to be an officer in the German army where he could boss people around, he jumped at the chance. (Ben Rubin, age 12)

Routes

Beginning the Journey

WITH YOUNGER CHILDREN (PRE-K–GRADE 2)

The library media specialist might wish to draw upon children's previous knowledge of villains from their bedtime stories. "Who is the meanest character in storybooks? Why did you pick that character? What was the meanest thing that character did? Why do you think the character acted that way? Greed? Revenge? Jealousy?" The library media specialist could then read aloud *The Three Little Pigs* (Marshall) and introduce several other books that portray the wolf as a villain. "What did the wolf do in *The Wolf Who Had a Wonderful Dream* (Rockwell)? In *Little Red Riding Hood* (de Regniers)? In *Peter and the Wolf* (Prokofiev)? Are the wolves in these books the same in any way? How are they different from each other? Which wolf is the meanest? Are any of the wolves humorous or sympathetic? Do real wolves behave like the wolves in these stories?"

Younger children may need to use both sound and movement to express their ideas and feelings. The library media specialist could invite children to take turns moving like a wolf, howling like a wolf. They could practice huffing and puffing and blowing down a cardboard house. They might want to create the scene in which the mother pig gives advice to her children as they go out into the world.

The group could be asked, "What is the mother feeling and thinking now? What are the little pigs feeling and thinking now?" The mother should warn them about the wolf and make a strong and vivid impression. Children might also want to create the scene where the wolf tries to persuade the first pig to open his door. Different wolves can use their own devices. They can try strange voices, disguises, flattery, trickery, or persuasion. They can follow the actual story line or improvise. Their goal is to be effective and sound sincere.

Each child could be asked to bring in a book featuring a strong villain. In a second session, the discussions and dramatizations could continue. A special collection of books featuring villains could be put on display. Children could also create their own "villain" books and illustrate them.

WITH MIDDLE GRADE CHILDREN (GRADES 3–5)

Middle grade children are ready for longer, more complex literary springboards. They are more able to understand motivation, to be empathetic. The library media specialist could tell the story of *Esther* (Chaiken) and have children analyze why Haman was such a powerful villain. Why was he so threatened by the new queen? Why was he suspicious of the Jews? Why did he feel so antagonized by Esther's cousin Mordecai? How did he try to influence the King?

The library media specialist could then engage children in the making of groggers or noisemakers, which they would rattle at the mere mention of Haman's name. Then one of the children could tell the story in his or her own words, and the others could do the booing and noisemaking. Children might enjoy making Hamantaschen, cookies shaped liked Haman's three-cornered hat. They can be filled with dates, raisins, and jellies. Some children might want to prepare and bake other treats tied to literary villains: the Wicked Queen's apple tarts, or troll house cookies shaped like the monster who waited under the bridge. They could use their original recipes and develop an illustrated cookbook.

WITH OLDER CHILDREN (GRADES 6-UP)

Older children can handle more sophisticated works and engage in more extensive discussions. They can focus with some depth on the complexity of the human character. The library media specialist might begin with a villain exam, a written test of general knowledge, given in the spirit of fun and community. Students are admonished to do their best and then asked to identify the names of famous literary villains: three evil witches from literature; three good witches from literature; three nasty storybook wolves; the two conspirators in *Robin Hood* (Pyle); the ambitious villainess in one of Shakespeare's greatest plays; the villain in *Tom Sawyer* (Twain); the troublemaker in *Alice in Wonderland* (Carroll); the one who makes life miserable for Little Orphan Annie; the beast who waits under the bridge; the big bully who is felled by a slingshot; the one who causes the destruction of King Arthur's Round Table;

the character who creates heartbreak in *Uncle Tom's Cabin* (Stowe); the troublemaker in Norse mythology; two bullies from Dr. Seuss's books; the characters who cause havoc in the *Yellow Submarine* (Dunning); the cunning villain in *The Jungle Book* (Kipling); three of the villains from "Batman"; the most ingenious adversary of Sherlock Holmes; Popeye's rival. The list is endless.

Children pool their knowledge and begin to define villains in sharing test results. Their collective thinking can provide a solid overview of the subject. The library media specialist should encourage debates and different points of view. ("I don't think Loki's a villain. He's just mischievous.") Each child could then be assigned to bring in two more questions about villains and bullies from other books and films. A second test could be created and given by these students to other students, and even to teachers (see fig. 5).

Excursions

VERBAL

"Persuasion Plays." Pairs of children improvise a variety of encounters involving villains: a child tries to dissuade the Grinch from stealing Christmas; a clever goat tries to persuade the troll to let her cross the bridge in peace; the Wicked Queen tries to persuade the mirror that she is the fairest of them all ("Just look at my complexion!"); a fly caught in a web tries to persuade a haughty spider not to eat her; Little Red Riding Hood's grandmother tries to persuade the wolf not to lock her in the closet ("I hate small, cramped places. I'm claustrophobic!"). These can be brought to life with all age groups.

"Press Conferences." Villainous storybook characters are urged to stay in character as they respond to a variety of questions posed by student journalists. In one session the Wicked Witch of the West was asked, "What do you think of Dorothy? How did you ever get involved with monkeys? Why do you have such an aversion to water? Do you do your shopping at the Emerald City? Do you find Oz to be a relaxing environment?"

"Courtroom Trials." At the trial of famous literary villains (Captain Hook, the Big Bad Wolf, Share Kahn, etc.), the prosecution and defense teams are given adequate time to develop their cases. Some children are assigned to be jurors, some to be witnesses. There could be a baliff, court reporter, and sketch artist. Other characters from the story might be called to the stand to give testimony. The trial preparation itself might take several sessions. A younger class could be invited for the day of decision:

> I am the lawyer, Rafael M. Cohen, defending my client, the Big Bad Wolf. He has been accused of blowing down the houses of the three little pigs and causing consider-

Villains and Bullies: Other Ways to Begin	Stories to Tell	Works to Read Aloud	Films to Share
Younger grades Pre-K–2nd	*Three Billy Goats Gruff* (Galdone)	*Crow Boy* (Yashima)	*Teeny-Tiny and the Witch Woman*
	Paper John (Small)	*Terrible Troll* (Mayer)	*Dragon's Tears*
	"The Chocolate That Turned to Stone" (Blackmore)	"The Old Lady Who Ate People" (Hinojoso)	*The Twelve Months*
Middle grades 3rd–5th	"Elsa and the Evil Wizard" (Phelps)	*Sara Crewe or What Happened at Miss Minchin's* (Burnett)	*Molly's Pilgrim*
	The Little Mermaid (Andersen)	*The Man Who Could Call Down Owls* (Bunting)	*Little Red Riding Hood: A Balinese-Oregon Adaptation*
	The Legend of Sleepy Hollow (Irving)	*Journey to Jo'bürg: A South African Story* (Naiido)	*Sounder*
Upper grades 6th–8th	"The Brocaded Slipper" (Vuong)	*The Devil's Arithmetic* (Yolen)	*To Kill a Mockingbird*
	"Body without Soul" (Calvino)	*Fly Free* (Adler)	*The Great Dictator*
	"The Old Woman and the Rice Cakes" (Phelps)	*The Chocolate War* (Cormier)	*Shane*

Fig. 5. Villains and Bullies: Other Ways to Begin

able property damage. I can prove that on that specific date and at those specific times my client was having severe allergy attacks. (Rafe Cohen, age 12)

"Debates." Cases could be developed pro and con as to whether various literary figures could be considered villains. (Was Ebenezer Scrooge a villain or just a crusty miser cut off from humanity? Was Captain Nemo a villain or a mad genius and protector of the sea?) Children should focus on defining their terms, knowing and understanding their character, and being persuasive.

Captain Nemo was a very lonely man because he had lost his wife and son. When people lose someone who was close to them, they do strange things. All Captain Nemo wanted to do was get rid of the people who killed his wife and son. Anybody under that much stress was bound to crash. ("The case for Captain Nemo," Asha Logan, age 11)

Captain Nemo resorted to violence before he tried anything else. He didn't want people to kill each other but he did so himself. He did what he claimed he was trying to prevent. Captain Nemo struck a ship that didn't even have any gun powder. He killed innocent men who were just doing an honest day's work. He was totally obsessed in his cause. ("The case against Captain Nemo," Paris Rutman, age 11)

WRITTEN

"Story Perspectives." This can involve all ages taking different, sometimes contradictory, points of view in a story. For example: the Golden Goose describes the Giant from her point of view; a rosebud in the Queen of Heart's garden describes the antics of the queen during the royal croquet game; a gold piece describes Fagin's gleefulness as he counts his treasure; the mirror describes the Wicked Queen.

Why does that Wicked Queen have to show up during my rest? I hate being her mirror. She's so demanding. She just won't leave me alone. I wonder if she ever gets tired of saying those same lines. Anyway, she's mad at me because I won't change my mind and say she is the fairest of them all. Life as a magic mirror isn't all that it is reflected to be. (Hillary Edwards, age 12)

"Imaginary Journals." What might readers discover if Moriarity or the Grinch kept a journal? Children could write two or three entries that would reveal the character's obsessions, plans, setbacks, feelings about others, and view of the world.

"Critical Incidents." The library media specialist describes an incident to a group of older children that involves a bully and another child. It might take place on a playground. There is a threatening mood. Children then write about what each of these two characters (bully and victim) is thinking and feeling during the incident.

"Spells, Chants, and Recipes." Children spend a session creating witches' spells, chants, and recipes for potions. There could be some discussion at first about the use of magical words or how one creates magical chants.

Twist and turn,
Blow and suck.
Make horses fly,
And people stuck.
(Hal Carlos Caylor, age 10)

A recipe for turning someone into a pear.

You will need these ingredients:
Three ground robin feathers.
Five drops of blood from a zoon.
Ten limes.
One drop of salt from the Red Sea.
One ground zoogo bug.

Put in dry ingredients. Stir, then boil for two years. Then add wet ingredients, and stir for eighty days. (Simone Lessac-Chenam, age 9)

"Film Reactions: *My Bodyguard* (Bill)." Films can trigger powerful and immediate discussions of a complete work. These are comments by fifth graders sparked by a contemporary film about a new boy standing up to a high school bully:

Bullies are motivated by other people's fear of them. They tell their victim what they will do if they don't obey. (Jade Dalton, age 11)

If you just fight back once, some bullies will be so startled that they will stop bullying. Also, you might ignore them which takes a lot of self-control. (Lucas Nivon, age 11)

Bullies are probably motivated by their parents. If their parents bully them, then they may do it to other people. Bullies are often very insecure. They pick on smaller and weaker people. They make you feel uncomfortable because you never think that you are safe. (Alex Corova-Nieto, age 11)

ART AND MUSIC

"Villains' Gallery." Children choose ten of their favorite villains and create "Most Wanted" posters that show their faces (caricatures) and list their heinous crimes. The posters should be bold and striking, and should be displayed in a "Villains' Gallery" or "Villains' Hall of Fame" (see fig. 6).

"Cartoons." A *New Yorker* cartoon once showed a perplexed Captain Hook waiting for his trunk at the airport. Children could develop other cartoons depicting literary villains dealing with the modern world, such as the Queen of Hearts exercising at a health club, the Big Bad Wolf trying to blow down a condominium, or Fagin using a bank card.

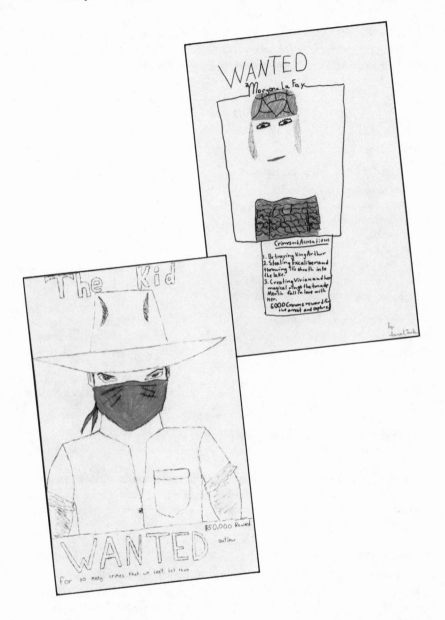

Fig. 6. Most Wanted Posters: "Morgan la Fay" (Sarah Tucker, age 11); "The Kid" (Jeff Hinson, age 11). Used with permission

"Games." Older children create a variation of the memory game for younger children. They would need to do some research to find out what characters would be fun and appropriate. There would need to be two sets of cards, one showing the heroes (for example, Hansel and Gretel), and one set featuring the villains (for example, the Witch). A symbol of the story (for example, the gingerbread house), would appear on both the hero and villain cards.

"Musical Villains." Students listen to a recording of *Peter and the Wolf* (Prokofiev) and are asked to identify the different characters by their musical instruments. The library media specialist could invite the music teacher to demonstrate one or more of the instruments used in this work. In the second session, children could be asked to link musical instruments to characters in other fairy tales. In *Jack and the Beanstalk* (Ross), for example, they would need to create the sounds for Jack, his mother, the cow, the Giant, and the Golden Goose.

"Musical Flourishes and Songs." The library media specialist gives a group of younger children some instruments (bells, drums, rhythm sticks) and has them create sounds and rhythms that would herald the entrance of a villain or beast. Children could learn some songs that deal with villains and monsters: "Abiyoyo"; "Ding! Dong! The Witch Is Dead"; "Who's Afraid of the Big Bad Wolf?"

RESEARCH

"Cultural Villains." Children expand their awareness of this theme by identifying villains in other cultures through the translations and adaptations of native folktales. They could then learn some of these tales and share them with their classmates. Examples of such villains would be "the Bunyip" (Cole) of Australia and "the Baba Yaga" (Cole) of Russia.

"Bullies' Collection." Children find and pull realistic fiction books that deal with the "bully" theme, and create a special collection for the library. Some possibilities: *Peter and Veronica* (Sachs), *The Bully of Barkham Street* (Stolz), *Wonder Kid Meets the Evil Lunch Snatcher* (Duncan), or *The Magic Book* (Roberts).

"Women Villains." Children, in their research, focus on female villains, who they were and what motivated them. They could choose either literary (Clytemnestra) or real life (Bonnie Parker) villains. They could also tackle issues of gender stereotyping. Why are there so many wicked stepmothers? How did this evolve? They could present their villains in the format of the "This Is Your Life" television show.

"Collective Bullies." Children investigate collective bullies (Nazis, Ku Klux Klan, South African government) and then develop a display exposing and documenting various acts of cowardice. The children might choose to convey their findings with a slide show or a video presentation.

Celebrations

"Bully Bingo." Younger children each receive a bingo board with sixteen blank squares. As the library media specialist calls out a specific character, object, or place, the children draw a picture of that item on their own boards, using any square they wish. Items might include a pumpkin creature, a spider's palace, the gingerbread house, the Troll's bridge, a ghost, the Wicked Queen's apple, a giant's footstep, an evil wizard's laboratory. This process is repeated seven more times. Students then obtain signatures from eight classmates to fill in the remaining eight squares. Then they are ready to play the game. Students must cover four squares in a row in order to win, calling out "Bully Bingo!" Much of the fun in this game is creating the playing board, an activity that can take up to thirty minutes.

"Villains' Processional." Children research the great villains in literature and then develop appropriate costumes. In a parade through the older classes, each villain takes the spotlight for a time and tells his or her tale. "I am the Phantom. I live in the belly of a great opera house in Paris. I have heard the voice of a divine soprano, and now I am obsessed by her music."

"The Villains' Auction House." Masters of villainy seek to raise funds by selling some of their most prized possessions to parents and teachers. Dressed in character, each villain takes turns conducting the bidding. Moriarity auctions Sherlock Holmes' fingerprinting kit. The Wicked Queen auctions off her mirror and poison apple recipe. The Giant offers his harp. The Big Bad Wolf auctions off the quilt from Grandma's bed. The money raised could go to purchasing books or videocassettes for the library.

"Bully Balladeers." Older children in masks and capes as a chorale group perform such poems as Alfred Noyes' "The Highwayman." They could travel to an older class, the teachers' lounge, neighborhood merchants, or a senior center. Occasionally they could pause to act out a scene. If they enjoy this experience, they could later in the year perform their version of "Jabberwocky" (Carroll).

A Journey Log: The "Pirate Curriculum"

I am walking along a misty dirt road at night, feeling weird. There is someone walking on the same side as me. The area has a slightly primeval mood. I switch sides, and so do the footsteps. I can see about five feet ahead. The footsteps draw closer. Suddenly, I turn around. A strong-looking woman steps out of the fog, and stops. She wears ragged clothes and her hair is tucked up in a knotted bandana. She wears a cutlass on one hip, and a long pistol on the other. She doesn't move, and at first I think she is a ghost. Then she sits down on a rotten stump and asks in a rough but friendly voice, "Who are you?" I am scared stiff but manage to stammer "Chrr, Chris." The woman explains that she's captain of the pirate ship *Rival*. "My real name is Rosemary but

everyone calls me Bloody Mary. I can't find my way back to port. Can you help me?''
(Chris Egleson, age 12)

STEP ONE: CHOOSING THE THEME

I chose the theme of "pirates" because it is romantic and theatrical. The world of pirates can be fresh terrain for children as it moves them away from the usual television fare and opens them up to new dramatic possibilities. It immediately evokes vivid pictures in their minds, stirring imaginations and offering opportunities for the creating and wearing of costumes. Role-playing as pirates can enable kids to feel powerful, to travel in vessels and own the Great Sea, to go on perilous quests for buried treasure. It can help to ease some of the fears in children, in this case their external fears of villains and bullies. They conquer the beast by becoming the beast. I also chose this theme because it was my first year at the school and I wanted to create the sense that the library could be a place for journeys, a place where children could spin their own tales and create their own worlds.

STEP TWO: PLANNING THE JOURNEY

The theme of "pirates" is universal, appealing to all age levels. I decided to pursue it with both younger and older groups, to hold sessions concurrently and provide an experience that would draw the two groups together. I chose the five- and six-year-old group and the nine- and ten-year-old group because of their jaunty character. These were the rogues of the school, mischief makers, pirates at heart, children with incredible spirit and ingenuity. Yet these were also children who often struggled and needed to have their energies channeled when they were together. Sessions with them could be exhilarating or devastating, and usually contained an element of risk or danger for the teacher.

I began my search through the collection to find related materials, especially picture books about pirates. I contacted teachers and friends to find particular song recordings. Most of my brainstorming occurred with two sixth grade library assistants who were almost experts on the subject of pirates. They spurred me on with their enthusiasm and acted as advisors throughout the journey. Several times they even stayed after school to help me prepare materials.

I met with each of the two head teachers. They, too, were genuinely excited about the idea of a "pirate curriculum." Already their children were filled with pirate visions, and the fives/sixes teacher showed how the younger ones sometimes swaggered into the meeting area and spoke in deep rumbling voices. Both teachers hoped that the "pirate curriculum" would allow their children to fantasize and be playful, channeling their anxieties and aggressive behaviors, and that this could serve to balance the hard academic work that was going on in both classrooms. Throughout this journey, they would share with me pirate anecdotes and any pirate spillover from the classroom. When I conceived the idea of a pirate academy as a final celebration for the pirate curriculum, again they were helpful and supportive. The nines/tens teacher volunteered to dress up as a pirate, and to be the principal of the Academy.

STEP THREE: BEGINNING THE JOURNEY (FIVES/SIXES)

The first session with the younger group began with an examination of a brightly colored pirate figure sculptured out of wood. I asked them what they knew about pirates. What did pirates wear? How did they speak? When did they live? Where did they live? They listened to me read aloud *One-Eyed Jake* (Hutchins) and *Anton B. Stanton and the Pirate* (McNaughton). They seemed to be particularly excited about pirate ships and pirate treasure.

STEP FOUR: TAKING SOME EXCURSIONS (FIVES/SIXES)

In a second session, I taught the students pirate language with homemade flash cards that matched archaic with contemporary words: yes/aye; no/nay; friend/matey; land ahead/land ho; wash the floor/swab the deck; oh, my goodness/shiver me timbers; pirate money/pieces of eight; pirate treasure/booty; pirate punishment/walk the plank; pirate drink/rum; pirate pet/parrot; boy/laddie; girl/lassie; here comes a whale/ thar she blows.

Working in pairs, students drew and cut out pirate ships and put them on a big mural of the sea. We talked a lot about the parts of a ship (mast, deck, crow's nest, hull, hatch). They chose their own pirate names, chose names for their ships, and made up stories about their sea journeys. We called our mural "The Crowded Sea."

In the third session, the children made pirate maps. They created keys for them and secret symbols. They each developed a set of directions. ("Start at the base of the fallen oak tree. Take three paces north toward Red Eye Gulch.") The maps were rolled up like scrolls and we hid them in different parts of the school as well as in special places in a nearby park.

During the fourth session, the five- and six-year-olds received a special delivery invitation to attend the Pirate Academy, where they could become authentic, official pirates with degrees. They were naturally quite excited. ("Will there be any homework?") We prepared by reviewing the flash cards, talking again about the parts of a ship, and adapting some sea songs ("What Shall We Do with the Drunken Pirate?"). We practiced our pirate penmanship, writing our pirate names with quill and ink on parchment paper. "We'll meet a week from today and attend the Academy," I reminded them. Anticipation was high.

STEP THREE: BEGINNING THE JOURNEY (NINES/TENS)

In my first session with the older group of nine- and ten-year-olds, I gave each student a palm-sized black paper circle. "What is this?" I asked, holding one up before me. "What could this mean? Why would this cause someone to shudder?" Everyone was curious, but most seemed perplexed. Finally, one girl began to chuckle. "It's the black spot," she declared. "It's from *Treasure Island* (Stevenson), and it means, "Death will come to you." This led to discussion about Long John Silver, Bluebeard, and Captain Kidd. Someone wondered if there were any lady pirates. We then pooled all our knowledge about pirate lore, and listed pirate characteristics on the board.

STEP FOUR: TAKING SOME EXCURSIONS (NINES/TENS)

I asked the students to imagine they were pirates, and then had them choose one of three questions to write about. "What's it like on the sea at night? What's it like during a storm? What's it like leaving someone behind?" They were encouraged to write with feeling and create a mood:

Peace. That's one word to describe the open sea at night. I think it's very beautiful with the stars and moon reflecting on the water. (Colin Perez, age 11)

I was spellbound watching over the princess all night. I was just an old pirate. I hadn't shaved in a week and my boots were scuffed. She was beautiful. She was wearing a silk pink dress with ruffles on the sleeves and lace around her neck. The water was calm. The moon was full. The light made her eyes look like emeralds. (Serena Chevere, age 11)

STEP FIVE: CELEBRATING THE JOURNEY (BOTH GROUPS)

During the second session, I introduced the idea of creating the Pirate Academy for the five- and six-year-olds. Would they want to be the instructors? If so, how would the Academy work (mechanics) and what would they teach (content)? I gave them a week to think it over. We spent the last thirty minutes collecting and searching through materials to find pirate information.

In the third session, these older children voted overwhelmingly in favor of creating the Academy. We decided on a format in which groups of three and four children would rotate from class to class for five-minute instructional sessions. All classes would be taught at the same time, enabling each small group to attend six different classes within the half hour time frame. The group chose specific content areas to be taught. Then the class broke into six groups and developed lessons. How would they introduce themselves? What specific skills, facts, or ideas did they want to impart? How could they make their sessions enticing? What props would they need? What should they do about costumes? How could they create a theatrical sense and provide some dramatic flair? We decided to ask the school director if we could hold the Academy in the music room, the school's most spacious area.

We spent the fourth session talking about working with younger children. How could we set a tone? How could we make the children feel at ease? As pirates, how could we stay in character and be robust yet gentle and not scare anyone? How could we help the children to feel successful and know that they would really be learning something? We practiced the "Drunken Pirate" song, which would open the Academy. Each small group then presented a lesson to the larger group, asking for feedback. "How can we improve our teaching? Did we stay in character?"

During free times that week, the nine- and ten-year-olds would come to the library to work on their costumes and props. Some made signs for their courses. Some made banners and giant ships to help change the look of the music room. I consulted many times with both head teachers to exchange information and anecdotes.

The fifth session, the Pirate Academy, was held jointly with both classes. As the five- and six-year-olds waited outside the music room, they were instructed to listen carefully to their new professors, the nines/tens. They began to hear singing from behind the music room door. The music was faint at first, then louder and more spirited.

The door opened and a lady pirate (the nines/tens teacher, Laura) appeared and introduced herself. She wore a red bandana and long dangling earrings. "To be a pirate you must think like a pirate." She asked them some questions. "What's 'Oh, my goodness' in pirate talk? How do you say, 'friend?' " She then led small groups of children to the six instructional areas. All of the courses began at the same time. The children seemed delighted by the look of the room: the giant ships, the most-wanted posters of famous pirates, the banners and flags and large treasure maps. After an intense five-minute learning session, the lady pirate would ring her cowbell and the groups would rotate to their next classes. By the end of the period, children had completed the following lessons:

"How to Polish Your Jewels." An instructor opened a broken treasure chest. "This jewel came from the island of Sardonia. This ruby was stolen from the Duchess of Versailles. This emerald is a phony. This bracelet once belonged to Captain Kidd." The other instructors provided tips on how to make your gems sparkle and the fives/sixes took turns polishing. They learned how to tell authentic jewels from fake jewels.

"How to Swab the Deck." The fives/sixes used actual mops and buckets of water to learn different cleaning methods. They took turns doing the "circular technique." One of the instructors explained the need for a shining ship. "No grime. There must be no grime." Another instructor would bellow from time to time, "A pirate is proud of his vessel!"

"How to Get Along with Your Parrot." One instructor introduced his puppet. "This is Shakespeare. He curses too much and talks too much but he recites some nice poetry. That's why I keep 'im." He then passed out kazoos and taught his class how to serenade a parrot. A second instructor explained about a parrot's disposition. "What should you do if your parrot acts stubborn or uppity? What is the proper parrot diet?"

"How to Move and Speak with Pirate Gusto." The fives/sixes took turns walking like pirates. They practiced the swagger. They recorded their voices into a tape machine. They attempted the pirate scowl, the laugh, the yawn. "Were you fierce and hearty, mateys? Did you make their bones chill? Did you make them want to walk on the other side of the street?" They then learned the words to "Fifteen Men on a Dead Man's Chest."

"How to Dress in Pirate Fashion." Instructors taught young pirates how to dress appropriately, how to use the eye patch and kerchief, how to coordinate colors, what to wear on a raid. "You have to have style, you know. People judge you by your appearance." One instructor demonstrated the proper use of the bandana. A lot of time was actually spent trying on different outfits. "That's you! I think it's perfect." The instructors always tried to give positive feedback.

"How to Walk the Plank." Young pirates were introduced to the pirate code of ethics. "You must never complain about the grub. You must never mention the word 'mutiny' when you are near the Captain's quarters. You must never be rude to the Captain's parrot. You must always say 'thank you' after robbing a lord or lady." They then spent time being blindfolded and experiencing the fear of coming close to the edge. As they walked the plank, they heard sea sounds and the shrieks of others waiting behind them.

After the last rotation, the student pirates and pirate instructors gathered to sing some pirate ditties and recite some pirate chants and oaths.

The sixth session, Graduation and Commencement, was held the next day. In a short ceremony, the newly trained pirates visited the library to receive their diplomas. The lights were dimmed to create a serious mood. Each child was called individually to receive his or her certificate. In the background, the Scalawag Choir (five sixth graders) were humming "Pomp and Circumstance." The young pirates glowed as each shared something that he or she learned at the Pirate Academy. Then they all recited the pirate oath.

I am a pirate, a true buccaneer.

I will at all times swab the deck, feed my parrot, and obey the laws of the sea.

The Scalawag Choir performed "Hoist Up the John B. Sails" and "Blow the Man Down." The graduates celebrated by eating biscuits and drinking (ginger) ale. The bottle labels were changed to read 1416. "That was a good year," someone toasted. "A very good year."

REFLECTIONS ON OUTCOMES

It was clear that all this pirate talk and all these pirate tales had enormous impact on the younger children and that they had become swept up in the stories and dramas, living them for a time. These were children who had to connect personally and then they would enter. The content had to touch their passions and concerns before something remarkable could happen. The pirate journey, at their demand, was to continue the following year. Almost every day, after these kids had moved into the sixes/sevens class, I would find between ten to twenty pirate notes hidden in the library, tucked into card catalog drawers and under the atlases. In one record-breaking day, I discovered forty-seven pirate warnings. There was still a waiting list for our seven pirate picture books, and a few of them were never returned.

That spring, I finally bowed to pressure and led the children and their teachers on a spying mission in Central Park. We crawled on our bellies near Devil's Hill where old pirates (sixth graders) came to rendezvous and reminisce. We witnessed them swap yarns and boast about their pieces of eight. And when they drank enough rum and fell to sleep, we snatched their treasure and ran for safety. This two-year journey laid the groundwork for other journeys in years to come. It enabled me to build a trusting, solid working relationship with the students. I could somehow spark their sense of adventure and they would always rise to the occasion.

The pirate study exposed the five- and six-year-olds to new authors and works as they listened to and browsed through a variety of picture books. They learned that pirate information could be obtained from all kinds of books and magazines. They began to understand the function of the card catalog and the encyclopedia. They developed a pirate vocabulary. They expanded their knowledge about the parts and working of a ship. They learned to read and draw maps and use symbols. They discovered who the most famous literary and real-life pirates were. They used their imaginations to become full-fledged pirate characters. Through this make-believe, they were perhaps able to overcome some of the anxieties and fears about bad guys and villains. Shy and quiet children had the chance to be boisterous. As they completed specific tasks at the Academy, they could feel accomplished and enjoy a sense of mastery. Their Pirate Academy certificate was something to cherish, a tangible reward for taking risks and coming on the journey.

The Pirate Academy was also one of the most constructive experiences for nine- and ten-year-olds that year. It eased some of the tensions and conflicts that were happening in their social group by providing them with a vehicle for working together and playing off each other. They were challenged in creating this world. They had to count on each other. Their strength as improvisers was tapped, building their confidence as a group and allowing them their moment in the sun. This was an area where they could shine, where they could reach out safely in costumes and guises. They were able to use their abilities again in creating a Comedy Museum as fifth graders and a Renaissance Faire while in the sixth grade.

The nine- and ten-year-olds also sharpened their research skills as they looked for pirate information, examining maps, photos and other graphics as well as the text. They learned the value of an index. They explored the role of pirates in literature, and why people were so attracted to them. What were they really like?

Were they scheming cutthroats or romantic renegades? What was the historical context in which they evolved? Who are the classical pirates in literature? In real life? What motivated them? Who are the pirates of today? They wrote original stories where the emphasis was on creating a mood.

The students learned about the dynamics of teaching. They chose specific content areas and developed a minicurriculum. They had to collect and organize material and work out effective ways to communicate their ideas. They had to consider the goal of the lesson. How could they make it a "hands on" experience? How could they create an inviting atmosphere? Why would it be important to have a sense of timing? They became aware of the developmental stages in looking at what five- and six-year-olds could handle and what they were capable of. What were the concentration skills? What would excite their curiosity? What might scare them? These important considerations forced them to become resourceful, independent problem solvers. In their role as teachers, they were empathetic to the younger children and sensitive to their struggles. "But one group, Gary, was so hard. They just couldn't listen." This comment struck close to home. We could tell they had also became more empathetic to their own teachers, having now walked in their shoes.

References

Books

Adler, C. S. *Fly Free.* Coward, 1984.

Andersen, Hans Christian. *The Little Mermaid,* ill. by Chihiro Iwasaki. Picture Book Studio, 1984.

Blackmore, Vivien. "The Chocolate That Turned to Stone" in *Why Corn Is Golden: Stories about Plants.* Little, 1984.

Bunting, Eve. *The Man Who Could Call Down Owls,* ill. by Charles Mikolaycak. Macmillan, 1984.

Burnett, Frances Hogson. *Sara Crewe or What Happened at Miss Minchin's.* Putnam, 1981.

Calvino, Italo. "Body without Soul" in *Italian Folk Tales.* Harcourt, 1980.

Carroll, Lewis. *Alice's Adventures in Wonderland,* ill. by Sir John Tenniel. St. Martin's, 1977.

———. *Jabberwocky,* ill. by Jane B. Zalben. Warne, 1977.

Chaiken, Miriam. *Esther,* ill. by Vera Rosenberry. Jewish Publication Society, 1987.

Cole, Joanna, ed. "The Baba Yaga" in *Best-Loved Folktales of the World.* Doubleday, 1982.

———. "The Bunyip" in *Best-Loved Folktales of the World.* Doubleday, 1982.

Cormier, Robert. *The Chocolate War.* Pantheon, 1974.

de Regniers, Beatrice Shenk. *Little Red Riding Hood,* ill. by Edward Gorey. Atheneum, 1972.

Duncan, Lois. *Wonder Kid Meets the Evil Lunch Box Snatcher.* Little, 1988.

Galdone, Paul. *The Three Billy Goats Gruff.* Clarion, 1979.

Hinojosa, Francisco. "The Old Lady Who Ate People" in *The Old Lady Who Ate People: Frightening Stories.* Little, 1984.

Hutchins, Pat. *One-Eyed Jake.* Greenwillow, 1979.

Irving, Washington. *The Legend of Sleepy Hollow,* retold by Robert D. San Souci, and ill. by Daniel San Souci. Doubleday, 1986.

Kipling, Rudyard. *The Jungle Book.* Grosset, 1959.

McNaughton, Colin. *Anton B. Stanton and the Pirate.* Doubleday, 1979.

Marshall, James. *The Three Little Pigs.* Doubleday, 1989.

Mayer, Mercer. *Terrible Troll.* Dial, 1968.

Naiido, Beverley. *Journey to Jo'biirg: A South African Story.* Lippincott, 1985.

Noyes, Alfred. *The Highwayman,* ill. by Charles Keeping. Oxford, 1981.

Phelps, Ethel J., ed. "Elsa and the Evil Wizard" in *The Maid of the North: Feminist Folk Tales from around the World.* Holt, 1981.

———. "The Old Woman and the Rice Cakes" in *Maid of the North: Feminist Folk Tales from around the World.* Holt, 1981.

Prokofiev, Sergei. *Peter and the Wolf,* retold by Patricia Crampton, and ill. by Josef Palecek. Picture Book Studio, 1987.

Pyle, Howard. *The Merry Adventures of Robin Hood.* Scribner's, 1946.

Remarque, Erich Maria. *All Quiet on the Western Front.* Little, 1958.

Roberts, Willo D. *The Magic Book.* Atheneum, 1986.

Rockwell, Anne. *The Wolf Who Had a Wonderful Dream.* Crowell, 1973.

Ross, Tony. *Jack and the Beanstalk.* Delacorte, 1981.

Sachs, Marilyn. *Peter and Veronica.* Doubleday, 1969.

Small, David. *Paper John,* Farrar, 1987.

Stevenson, Robert Louis. *Treasure Island.* Macmillan, 1963.

Stolz, Mary. *The Bully of Barkham Street.* Harper, 1963.

Stowe, Harriet Beecher. *Uncle Tom's Cabin.* Modern Library, 1985.

Twain, Mark. *The Adventures of Tom Sawyer.* Macmillan, 1962.

Vuong, Lynette Dyer. "The Brocaded Slipper" in *The Brocaded Slipper and Other Vietnamese Tales.* Lippincott, 1982.

Yashima, Taro. *Crow Boy.* Viking, 1955.

Yolen, Jane. *The Devil's Arithmetic.* Viking, 1988.

Films

Dragon's Tears. McGraw-Hill, 1962. 6 min.

The Great Dictator, dir. by Charlie Chaplin. United Artists, 1940. 128 min.

Little Red Riding Hood: A Balinese-Oregon Adaptation. Films, Inc., 1980. 17 min.

Molly's Pilgrim. Phoenix, 1985. 24 min.

My Bodyguard, dir. by Tony Bill. Fox, 1980. 96 min.

Shane, dir. by George Stevens. Paramount, 1953. 117 min.

Sounder, dir. by Martin Ritt. Fox, 1972. 105 min.

Star Wars, dir. by George Lucas. Fox, 1977. 121 min.

Teeny-Tiny and the Witch Woman. Weston Woods, 1982. 14 min.

To Kill a Mockingbird, dir. by Robert Mulligan. Universal-International, 1962/ 129 min.
The Twelve Months. Coronet, 1980. 11 min.
Yellow Submarine, dir. by George Dunning. Great Britain, 1968. 85 min.

Recordings and Songs

"Abiyoyo" in *Pete Seeger's Greatest Hits* (audio recording). Columbia, 1967.
"Blow the Man Down" in *The Fireside Book of Folk Songs*. Simon and Schuster, 1947.
"Ding! Dong! The Witch Is Dead!" in *The Wizard of Oz*. Selections from original soundtrack. Words and music by E. Y. Harburg and H. Arlen. MGM, 1956.
"Drunken Sailor" in *The Fireside Book of Folksongs*. Simon and Schuster, 1947.
"The John B. Sails" in *Hard Traveling*, sung by Cisco Houston (audio recording). Folkways, 1954.
Peter and the Wolf, composed by Sergei Prokofiev and performed by London Symphony Orchestra (audio recording). Angel SFO, 1973.
"Who's Afraid of the Big Bad Wolf" in *The Walt Disney Songbook*. Golden, 1971.

The Second Journey: Humor

Introduction to the Study

Humor is personal and experiential and must touch a child's reality. There is a certain mastery required in "getting" a joke, and it depends, to some extent, on a child's cognitive level. Humor provides children with a way of working through their anxieties. It allows them to discharge and manage their aggression and express their forbidden impulses. It offers them a language in which they can engage others and build friendships.

Humor can help to create or change a mood. It can bring material to life in fresh and pleasurable ways. It can break the ice, alleviate boredom, and contribute to a warm, positive tone. It is infectious, a source for bonding. It allows children to see a grownup's humanity.

The use of humor in the classroom can be powerful and telling. Humor can be a measure for knowing someone's intelligence, perceptiveness, sensitivity, and imagination. The teacher who knows this one quality in a child knows something about that student's sense of self and sense of the world. When the library media specialist first laughs with a student, it is like breaking bread with that child. All of a sudden, they glimpse one another's inner being. After that, they view each other differently.

Children rarely get a feeling for the humor of a people in historical studies. What made them laugh? What was the character of their humor? Was it bawdy? Was it subdued? Even though humor mirrors the concerns of a culture, it is often the extraordinary missing piece. Humor is the element that can give flavor to a study and make it vital and connective.

Who are the humorous authors and illustrators? What is unique about their styles? James Stevenson uses the format of a grandfather reminiscing to spin his fantastic yarn in *Could Be Worse*. William Steig can be richly satirical in such books as *The Real Thief*. How do both their texts and illustrations contribute to the nonsense, each in special ways? Daniel Pinkwater blends humor with science fiction in *Fat Men from Space*. Jack Prelutsky can use monstrous imagery and still remain funny in *Nightmares*.

Discussions can center on what makes a story funny. Is it a character? The plot? The dialogue? Do children laugh because they identify with a situation or because the writing is so absurd or nonsensical? How can humor establish the point of view of a book? How can humor provide balance or comic relief?

Humor can be approached through characterization. Why do certain characters seem funny? *Curious George* (Rey) amuses with his mischievousness. *The Emperor's New Clothes* (Andersen) and *Yertle the Turtle* (Seuss) are funny because they are so arrogant. *Pierre* (Sendak) is outrageous and defiant. *Amelia Bedelia* (Parish) is so literal. *The Lady Who Saw the Good Side to Everything* (Tapio) is almost obnoxiously upbeat. Holden Caulfied in Salinger's *Catcher in the Rye* is irreverent.

Humor can be approached through a particular subject. For example, food is a terrific source for comical situations and dramatic possibilities. Nursery rhyme characters like Jack Horner, Little Miss Muffet, and Jack Sprat all have problems relating to food. Folktales, such as *The Little Red Hen* (Galdone) and *The Gingerbread Boy* (Galdone) provide both humor and moral teachings. In *Strega Nona* (dePaola), there is too much pasta. *Homer Price* (McCloskey) produces too many doughnuts. Just preparing soup can lead to catastrophic results in *The Teeny Tiny Woman* (Seuling) and *The Tailypo* (Galdone).

What is peculiar or unique about American humor? It can be exciting to expose children to the tall tales and whoppers that are an integral part of American folklore. They could examine "exaggeration" as a key element in this kind of humor. They could see how fabricating and stretching the truth can be developed into an art form if one has a keen imagination and strong sense of bravado.

Children need to understand why people laugh even when something's not funny. They laugh at times when they feel anxious or uncomfortable. They laugh in order to belong or to be accepted. They laugh to seem congenial or project an image. The "class clown" may feel pressure to make wisecracks all the time.

Humor can have an edge. It can be provocative. It can sting. It can be directed against a person or a group. A practical joke can go too far. Teasing can become competitive. If someone crosses the line, the humor can turn sour and acidic. Bantering can turn to baiting.

When groups are oppressed, humor can provide relief and fellowship. It can get someone through a day, allow moments of escape, and lighten a grim reality. Black humor and Jewish humor are distinctive examples of survival humor. Both groups have been put down, attacked, and rejected by the mainstream culture at one time or another. Humor and pain are rooted together, reflecting different facets of the same experience.

A thematic study of humor provides a rich vocabulary to explore. What is irony? In "The Ransom of Red Chief" (Henry), the kidnappers get more than they bargain for when they have to deal with an impossibly obnoxious kid. This twist sets up most of the story's humor. Other words include "comedy," "spoof," "parody," "satire," "farce," "pun," "deadpan," "nonsense," "slapstick," "guffaw," "belly laugh," "funny bone," "comic relief," and "canned laughter." Older children might delight in learning some of such wonderfully descriptive Yiddish words as "yenta," "clutz," and "chutzpah."

Humor can be a strength, a gentling force. Being able to laugh at oneself can move someone closer to self-awareness. Humor can help someone to heal or at least cope with trying times. It is also a language, a language that children enjoy and speak often. If their humor is valued, grownups can enter their world and see what is important to them.

Routes

Beginning the Journey

WITH YOUNGER CHILDREN (PRE-K–GRADE 2)

The library media specialist could begin by reading aloud Judi Barrett's *Cloudy with a Chance of Meatballs,* a nonsensical book about a land where the weather changes three times a day and it can even rain pancakes and syrup. There are many questions to explore in subsequent discussions. "Would you like to live in Chewandswallow? What foods would you like it to rain? What foods would you not like it to rain? How would you describe the Gingerbread House discovered by Hansel and Gretel? How would you describe Willie Wonka's chocolate factory? What can happen when there is too much of a good thing? Why is *Cloudy with a Chance of Meatballs* such a funny story?"

Children then create a three-dimensional map of a fantasy land where all the streets and neighborhoods are related to food. "Who might you see walking down Cucumber Court? What would the cars look like? Describe the houses, the landscape, the playgrounds." Working individually or in pairs, students design and animate their section of the map. A sample of possible streets and areas: Asparagus Alley, Lasagna Lane, Bon Bon Boulevard, Strawberry Street, Deli Drive, Tomato Terrace, Pistachio Park, Watermelon Way. Some children might enjoy making up imaginary addresses, labeling them on the map, and giving directions to their houses. "I live at 110 Pumpkin Place, just south of Rum Cake Road."

WITH MIDDLE GRADE CHILDREN (GRADES 3–5)

The library media specialist tells a love story such as *Perez and Martina* (Belpré) or *The Frog Prince* (Galdone) in a sentimental voice and then invites children to act out scenes from the story.

Children then create old-fashioned love boxes, pink and frilly, that could be sent to different classrooms around the school, perhaps during Valentine's week, to bring some joy during the winter doldrums. Included in these boxes might be miniature heart-shaped people, clothespin cupids, recipes for lovedrop cookies, lyrics to old-time heart songs ("You've Got to Have Heart"), chocolate kisses, and bracelets made with wire and red beads.

Students devise a love test in which the players would have to match some famous romantic pairs who are always linked together: Popeye/Olive Oyl; Clark Kent/Lois Lane; Robin Hood/Maid Marian; Julius Caesar/Cleopatra; Romeo/Juliet; George/Martha; Ralph/Alice; Tom Sawyer/Becky Thatcher; Tramp/Lady; Fred/Ginger; Tony/Maria.

Children could create their own stories about the power of Cupid's arrow and the sometimes wild consequences:

> There was once a girl named Molly. One day she was walking by the frog pond in her garden. Suddenly, she felt a little prick and at that moment, she saw a most particular frog. It was emerald green and she fell madly in love with it. Molly just sat there saying very romantic things to the frog. The frog would just sit and listen to her. This went on all summer. Most people thought it was a silly romance but Molly didn't care. ("Lovestruck," Rebecca Bleichman, age 11)

WITH OLDER CHILDREN (GRADE 6-UP)

The library media specialist begins by playing the Allan Sherman parody, "Camp Granada." What images does this song evoke? "I went diving with Joe Spivey. He developed poison ivy. Camp is very entertaining, and they say we'll have some fun if it stops raining." What are the humorous moments that contribute to making the experience of sleepaway camp so vivid and affecting?

The library media specialist then introduces three novels that bring this experience to life: Herman Wouk's *City Boy,* Ellen Conford's *Hail! Hail! Camp Timberwood,* and Paula Danziger's *There's a Bat in Bunk Five.* How do such offbeat characters as Herbie Bookbinder survive in this new, strange, and self-contained world? Do they make friends? Do they simply endure or do they triumph? How do they use humor as a strength? How do they deal with so many kinds of personalities, new routines and rituals, and being so very far from home?

Students form small work groups to develop and perform skits incorporating some of the comical and quirky elements of camp life: bug juice, homesickness, campfires, learning to dive, canteens, mail call, counselors, night hikes, daddy longlegs, flashlights, parents' visiting day, sleepouts, frog catching, and snipe hunts.

Working individually, children write fictitious letters home. Children, in pairs or small groups, could design and discuss their ideal camp. ("You wake up at 10:30. The counselor makes your bed. You have fritos and chocolate cake for morning snack") (see fig. 7).

Humor: Other Ways to Begin	Stories to Tell	Works to Read Aloud	Films to Share
Younger grades Pre-K–2nd	"Why Dogs Hate Cats" (Lester)	*Pigs in Hiding* (Dubanevich)	*Madeline*
	What's So Funny Ketu? (Aardema)	*Meanwhile Back at the Ranch* (Noble)	*People Soup*
	Turnabout (Wiesner)	*The Dunkard* (Selden)	*The Chicken*
Middle grades 3rd–5th	"The Wolf, the Fox, and the Jug of Honey" (Belpré)	*Skinnybones* (Park)	*Gerald McBoing-Boing*
	The Children of Chelm (Adler)	*Rolling Harvey down the Hill* (Prelutsky)	*Pigbird*
	"Talk" (Courlander)	*The Whipping Boy* (Fleischman)	*The Court Jester*
Upper grades 6th–8th	"Three Strong Women" (Phelps)	*Dorrie's Book* (Sachs)	*Munro*
	"Zlateh the Goat" (Singer)	*One Fat Summer* (Lipsyte)	*Cooley High*
	"The Night the Bed Fell" (Thurber)	*I Tell a Lie Every So Often* (Clements)	*Hope and Glory*

Fig. 7. Humor: Other Ways to Begin

Excursions

VERBAL

A number of amusing folktale improvisations can be introduced to all ages, using the familiar repertory of characters.

"Lost and Found." A lost and found worker encounters various folktale characters during the course of a morning. Patient and respectful, he or she tries to obtain information about the specific lost treasure or possession. "Describe it. When did you last see it? What does it mean to you? What is its actual worth?" Among those interviewed might be: Jack, who has lost a magic bean; the Wicked Queen, who has lost her poison apple recipe; the Giant, who has lost his harp; Rapunzel, who has lost her comb and brush set; Geppetto, who has lost his hammer; or the Wicked Stepsisters, who have lost their invitation to the ball.

"Real Estate." A real estate agent attempts to sell prospective buyers one of the homes in Fairy Tale Village. The agent needs to be persuasive and focus on important features and property values. ("It's a very nice neighborhood.") Homes might include: Rapunzel's tower; the First Pig's straw house; Peter's pumpkin shell; the Troll's bridge; the Giant's castle ("It's quite spacious"); Humpty Dumpty's wall; or the Old Lady's shoe ("Perhaps you'd prefer a sneaker").

"Promises, Promises." Fairy tale characters running for mayor of Fairy Tale Village present their political platforms. Little Red Riding Hood promises a basket of goodies for everyone, a lighted path through the forest, and a wolf recognition course for children. Pinocchio promises free puppet shows and truth-telling kits. The Second Little Pig promises better housing. Hansel promises free gingerbread and a witch removal service. The Oldest Stepsister makes a special pitch for the women's vote:

> What do you want for tomorrow's generation? Do you want your daughters going to dances with dresses from Woolworth's? No! You want to buy them Cinderella originals. They're lacy. They're lovely. They're yours when you vote for me. (Serene Chevere, age 11 and Donnette Smalls, 11)

"Fairy Tale Twists." These are some "what if" situations that could have changed the lives of fairy tale characters, and the happy-ever-after endings as well. For example: the Princess spends an uncomfortable night sleeping on a squash; Cinderella gets caught in a traffic jam (there are just too many coaches on the road—"Isn't there anything you can do?" she pleads to her coachman); Jack gets detained when he tries to borrow an axe from his chatty neighbor ("So how's your mother, Jack? I hear there were some problems with the cow. Would you like some tea?").

"Detective Spoofs." Children develop characters and skits that spoof the Encyclopedia Brown series (Sobol). Dictionary Jones could have a special way with words, always defining them and breaking them down. Almanac Ike might zero in on weather facts and conditions. Atlas Annie could focus on geographical concerns, interpreting clues in terms of longitude and latitude.

WRITTEN

"Barnyard Blues." The library media specialist reads aloud to younger children *The Day Jimmy's Boa Ate the Wash* (Noble). This humorous story presents a wild chain of events that occurs when a class takes a field trip to a farm. Children could then dictate or write their own stories about the "barnyard blues." ("There's trouble on the farm!")

There was once a farmer who milked a cow by his tail. He ate all the pigs' food, and rode horses backwards. And once he tried to grow his daughter in the garden. (Sean Neal, age 7)

Once there was a happy farmer. The animals were happy, too, but one day the animals went on strike. The chickens wanted a television. The cows wanted to live in a mansion. The pigs wanted rich French foods. (Kimberly Bowman, age 8)

"Animal Lectures." Children pretending to be animal professors prepare and give their first lecture of the school year. They should think about content and how to excite their students and create a positive tone.

Hi. My name is Anansi the spider. I am going to teach you how to make a web, and where to make it. I have over one hundred webs. My father is a Daddy Long Legs. My mommy is a Mother Short Legs. The best place to make a web is in the shade of an oak tree. (Jonzi Jiminez, age 9)

Hello, my fellow cats. My name is Doctor Leroy Cat and I will be teaching you what to do when you retire and you are too old to chase mice. I shall teach you how to beg for food. Go to a city street, sit by a building, and moan sadly. If you are good, someone will take you home and feed you. (Anne Woodman, age 9)

"Fantastic Pet Stories." The library media specialist reads some *Whoppers* (Schwartz) or *Ten Tall Tales* (Bird) and then has children concoct their own fantastic pet stories. They should be encouraged to think big and use exaggeration:

There was once a man named Billy Joe and he was a wild hunter. One night he heard a wolf howling. "Gosh!" he said. "I want that wolf." He grabbed his gun and ran outside to get him. He chased that wolf for fourteen years, through forests and mountains, and long tangled trails. He chased him up hills and down hills and through dingles and dales. When he finally caught up, the wolf cried, "Mercy! I can't run anymore." Billy Joe took him home and taught him to sing. (Sarah Tucker, age 9)

"My Wild and Daring Mom." *The Man Whose Mother Was a Pirate* (Mahy) can stimulate children to create humorous fictional tales about their groundbreaking moms who work in unusual professions. Their moms might be ringmasters, spies, skyriders, archaeologists, deep-sea divers, championship bowlers. In later discussions, the group could explore how gender stereotyping has at times curtailed women's involvement in numerous risk-taking fields.

My mom is a deep sea fisher. She goes diving a lot and has a harpoon gun. I sometimes go, too. She brings salmon, tuna, flounder, swordfish, and shark home for dinner and sells the rest. I get tired of fish, because my bed is stuffed with mackerel. (Gabriel Evansohn, age 7)

My mom is a witch. Everyday she makes a spell. She cackles with joy and, for breakfast, she makes me blue French toast. My mom takes me out on her broom with our cat, Scratcher. She spins around and goes upside down. This makes me fall off, but every time she catches me. (Nicole Letelier, age 9)

My mom is a swell firefighter. She practices with a long leaf blower and a bunch of ripped up paper. You think your mom wakes you up early. My mom gets me up at 3 o'clock and goes over fire rules. All my clothes are red, and I have no sneakers, only boots. When we go out, she makes me wear a fire hat that droops over my eyes. The only dog I'm allowed to have is a Dalmatian. (Brian Cintron, age 12)

"Film Reactions." The following are reactions to *Stalag 17*, the 1950s comedy classic directed by Billy Wilder. It effectively depicts how prisoners of war use humor to ease their suffering and combat their boredom.

I think that the scene that revealed someone's character was the one where Animal was looking at pictures of Betty Grable, and you could see that he was really suffering because he was without a woman, and he just wanted to have a good time and he was being deprived of things that he really enjoyed. (Chloe Tribich, age 11)

The P.O.W.s had to be resourceful to stay alive. They all had to use certain things to have any fun at all. They used little bits of scrap to make musical instruments. Septon (the William Holden character) was the most resourceful out of all of them. Since they couldn't watch and bet on horse races, Septon made it so that they could bet on little mouse races. He also made a telescope so that they could look into the Russian women's bathroom. (Ethan Nichtern, age 12)

"The First Laugh." Children imagine a stark world of caves and wild beasts and then conjecture about the earliest people. What would a day be like? What funny things could have happened during the course of a day? What might have caused the first laugh? What was the first joke? What was the first riddle?

Once upon a time, a cave man moved his fingers against his ribs. A ticklish, happy feeling swept over him. He began to make weird sounds. Hearing him, all the other cave people ran out to see him, and they began to move their fingers against their ribs. Imitating him, they began to get better and better at it, until, joy to the world, laughter was born. (Allen Wilson, age 12)

ART AND MUSIC

"Inventing Letters." Dr. Seuss's *On Beyond Zebra* could inspire students to invent new letters of the alphabet:

"JWJ." This letter is called the glosher. I use it to spell "gloshula." A gloshula has only one tooth in the front of its mouth. It always looks up. Gloshulas eat spinach and spaghetti sauce. They are very shy and live in groups of three. (Remy Chait, age 8)

"Droodles." Children could create picture riddles as described in *Unriddling* (Schwartz) (see fig. 8).

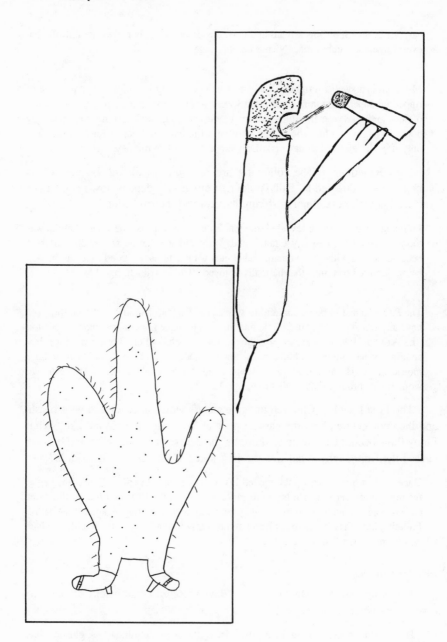

Fig. 8. Droodles: "A Singing Microphone" and "A Tap Dancing Cactus" (Steven Escobar, age 9). Used with permission

"Animal Fashion Shows." After listening to *Animals Should Definitely Not Wear Clothing* (Barrett), children design and make fashions for cutout cardboard animals. They could even create a fashion show with a fabric runway. Certain children might want to provide a running commentary.

"Parodies." Children listen to records by Allan Sherman and Al Yankovich and then create their own parodies. They could poke fun at school life, family life, current events, and the sports, music, and movie worlds.

"Mini-Operas." Children develop musical dramas from their favorite nursery rhymes or fairy tales, singing their lines and gesturing dramatically. Little Miss Muffett could carry on endlessly about her woes. The spider could sing an apology.

RESEARCH

"A Joke and Riddle Collection." Younger children examine their own school library collection to see where the joke and riddle books are kept. They could share the material from these books with each other and then develop their own joke and riddle books for a special classroom collection.

"Early Television Broadcasting." Older students might enjoy doing research about the early days of television, when broadcasts were live and the medium was more spontaneous. Who were television's earliest clowns? What were some of the problems and pitfalls they encountered? An exciting project might involve kids obtaining old television scripts of such shows as Sid Caesar's "Your Show of Shows," "I Love Lucy," or "The Honeymooners." Some of these scripts could be read aloud or dramatized in a recreation of a live comedy show from the 1950s. Members of the crew might include actors, producers, special effects artists, makeup artists, set designers, camera technicians, and someone to warm up the audience. *A Pictorial History of Television* (Settel and Laas) is a good introduction to television history.

"Court Jester Study." Some students could do historical studies about court jesters. How were individuals chosen for this role, and how did they learn and develop their art? Why were individuals with disabilities (dwarfs, hunchbacks, etc.) sometimes chosen? Students could try to find out what influence jesters have had on kings and queens and how they were perceived by members of the royal court. Did only European countries have court jesters? Students, dressed in costumes, could then perform some tricks and routines to class members.

"The Fool in Folktales." Some children may want to examine the role of the fool in folktales. They could research stories from all over the world and pull those tales in which the fool has an important role. Does the fool only provide comic relief, or is he or she sometimes the wisest person? Does he or she ever win the hand of the prince or princess and emerge as the story's hero? The children might then want to dramatize some of these stories, create their own works, or even sponsor a "festival of fools."

Celebrations

"A Post Office." *The Jolly Postman or Other People's Letters* (Ahlberg) might inspire students to design stamps, make envelopes, and send jokes, riddles, limericks, and phony invitations to various staff members or classes in the school. They might want to cancel some nonexistent fictional events such as Mother Goose's tupperware party or Little Jack Horner's bake sale.

"A Pan Festival." Children could act out stories about the Greek god Pan, who was almost always engaged in raucous noisemaking and humorous pranks. *Tales of Pan* (Gerstein) is a perfect sourcebook and contains thirteen illustrated stories. Students could dress in sheets and olive wreaths for the festival, and feast on moussaka and little Greek salads.

"The Wild West." In the spirit of Steven Kellogg's retelling of the *Pecos Bill* legend, children might create a Wild West town. The town could be populated with blacksmiths, pony express riders, temperance workers, cattlemen, rodeo stars, and miners. There might be special events like riding a bronco or panning for gold. Two old desert rats could spin a variety of cactus tales in a puppet show. A coyote choir might perform a Western medley.

A Journey Log: The "Comedy Curriculum"

One day I was walking by my pond and found a frog. I picked it up and took it inside my house. I filled up my bathtub with water and put in the frog. I then tried to teach it how to dance. Pretty soon, it got the hang of it. I taught it how to hip dance. I put a skirt on it and a feathered hat. It became very rich and went on tours. (Safiya Raheem, age 9)

STEP ONE: CHOOSING THE THEME

The theme of humor is a natural one for engaging children and drawing them in. It can also be a lifesaver in difficult situations. The library was being renovated and was unavailable for program use during the year of this study. Books were stored away in boxes and I was teaching in twelve different locations. Obviously, we needed some laughter to endure, and a comedy curriculum seemed like the perfect content for students, teachers, and especially for me. I was also looking for a strong follow-up project for the fifth graders who had excelled as founders of the Pirate Academy the year before.

STEP TWO: PLANNING THE JOURNEY

This was to be one of my first full partnerships with a head teacher in designing and implementing a curriculum. Cynthia, the fifth grade teacher, seemed enthusiastic about exploring this theme. During our planning, she brought imaginative ideas and a rich knowledge of her age group. The two of us focused on both content and the needs and struggles of individual kids. In fact, we spent considerable time working out combinations of kids for small group work that might lead to productive results. This teacher very much enjoyed the playful dimension, performing, improvising, bantering with kids. She was both dynamic and relaxed, willing to be a part of the journey wherever it moved. Her input was immense. She helped to center things and to sustain the journey with her warmth and steadiness.

STEP THREE: BEGINNING THE JOURNEY

In the first session, we explored the importance of jokes to families, and how they got passed down from generation to generation. ("What is the first joke you remember hearing?") We spent some time having a "joke-athon" and practiced developing a sense of timing and delivery. ("How do you tell a joke effectively?") We examined the parts of a joke: the setup, the body, and the punchline. I introduced students to a tape of Abbott and Costello's "Who's on First?" and we listened carefully to the delivery to determine why this routine is considered such a classic.

STEP FOUR: TAKING SOME EXCURSIONS

We looked at and discussed the comedy prototypes. Who were these all-time players one might encounter in any corner of the world? The know-it-all, who is just waiting to put her foot in her mouth; the wiseguy, who tries to turn everything into a joke; the busybody, who is always gossiping and willing to impose his wisdom and advice; the misfit, who sees the world as an outsider and may often have a poignant quality; the snob, the slob, the pessimist, the complainer, the rogue, the gung-ho enthusiast.

Cynthia and I set up improvisations so that some of these universal characters could interact with each other in all kinds of contexts: riding on a stagecoach in the Wild West; building pyramids for the Pharaoh; buying and selling in a Greek marketplace; preparing a banquet for King Arthur; visiting a Chicago speakeasy in the Roaring Twenties.

We expanded the second session to two hours. We presented a tape of *When I Was a Kid*, some of Bill Cosby's stories about his growing up in Philadelphia. We discussed his style, content, and delivery. The group concluded that Bill Cosby was a warm and gentle storyteller who caught the humor of everyday rituals and adventures.

We watched *The Gold Rush*, and explored the magic of Charlie Chaplin's comedy style. Why do we feel so much for his character? The group concluded that his humor was visual, poetic, graceful, and from the heart. We focused on the famous scene where he is eating his shoe. Why is this scene so funny and believable?

At the end of the session, we assigned each person to choose a comedian and bring in any background material and examples of the comedian's work, including tapes, records, scripts, biographies, and other writings. Each student was to be prepared to introduce their comedian and define his or her style.

Cynthia and I began the third session by sharing with the class some of the comedians that we were most excited about: Ernie Kovacs, who was inventive and experimental with props; Will Rogers, who was so insightful as a political humorist; Mae West, who was tough and sassy and always had a good time; Lenny Bruce, whose genius was consumed by rage; Judy Holliday, who masked her wisdom and intelligence with a "dumb blonde" persona.

As students presented their comedians, they began to see that it was not always easy to define a specific comedy style, that comedy was personal, and comics struck different chords in different people. ("I don't see what's so funny about him.") We were able to characterize Woody Allen as a nebbish, Jackie Gleason's Ralph Kramden as a loudmouth, Peter Sellers' Inspector Clouseau as an arrogant fool, and the Marx Brothers as nutty jesters running amok in the world.

STEP FIVE: CELEBRATING THE JOURNEY

In the last part of our session, we began to plan a comedy museum as a vehicle for sharing our ideas and materials with others in the school. How could we make this museum a funny place? How could we give others a sense of comedy history and of different comedy styles? Cynthia and I divided the students into pairs and small groups of three and four, and they chose areas of humor and comedy that had special interest for them to develop into centers. We began working on prop lists, creating original routines, and painting and drawing signs.

In the fourth session, we met as a class. Each pair and group presented its specific ideas about what the younger children would do at its center. ("This is how we will begin. These will be our activities. We will demonstrate this. We will perform this. We will teach them this. These will be our costumes. These will be our props. This is how we will close.")

The fifth and sixth sessions were intensive work periods spent scavenging, painting, writing, practicing routines. Cynthia and I floated around helping children focus on details and think through their presentations.

The Comedy Museum was held in the fifth grade classroom. To enter the Museum, each seven- and eight-year-old had to bring a joke or riddle from home written on an index card. These cards served as their passports to the comedy centers.

"The Special Props Exhibit." Two tour guides demonstrated how to play a few notes on Harpo Marx's harp and Jack Benny's violin. They let the younger children try on some of Milton Berle's wigs and Red Skelton's baggy pants. They showed the children a script from the Carol Burnett show and the bucket used by her charwoman character. "This is a postcard Lucy sent to Fred and Ethel." All of the artifacts had big labels and written descriptions. "This is Ralph Kramden's bowling ball. Do you want to lift it?"

"The Old Time Comedy Shop." The seven- and eight-year-olds made Groucho Marx moustaches out of tape and construction paper. They learned how to walk like Groucho Marx and how to roll their eyes. They learned how to do the Jack Benny "double take" and how to speak like W. C. Fields. Those who wanted could create original playlets with handsome Punch and Judy puppets.

"Clown School." The sevens/eights were taught in pantomime how to give an elephant a bath, how to wake a lion from a nap, and how to mimic the ring-master. They could also practice juggling with real balls and put on authentic clown makeup.

"Ventriloquism 101." Students were taught how to throw their voices and project sounds with a Charlie McCarthy dummy. The more advanced students got to practice "double-talk"—how to speak quickly and say nothing. The instructors here were especially patient. ("Talk through the sides of your mouth.")

"The Tall Tale Center." Each child had the opportunity to spin a whopper to explain why he or she was late to school. Children were encouraged to look "poker-faced" and speak earnestly. "Make it fantastic!" Then the fifth graders spun wild tales about their various pets: a sheepdog who could do the mambo; a chicken who liked to rollerskate; a gibbon who never lost a game of checkers; a hummingbird who could hum all of Mozart's operas.

"The Mad Tea Party." Children were introduced to Alice, the Mad Hatter, the March Hare, and the Dormouse. They soon became engaged in a whirlwind of activity, drinking tea, toasting one another, and eating tea cakes. Every few minutes, the characters switched places and sang the "Very Merry Unbirthday" song. They were always asking the same silly riddles. "Why is a marble like a chicken? Why is a chicken like a chicken?" From time to time, a grumpy Queen of Hearts would pop in and demand to know, "Who painted my roses red?"

"The Dial-A-Joke Booth." The sevens/eights could enter a giant windowed cardboard box and dial on a plastic play phone. They could dial "J" for joke, "R" for riddle, or "L" for limerick. A cheery voice from outside the box would talk with them. But sometimes they might get the operator who spoke in the shrillest, most nasal tone. "You have dialed incorrectly. Do not dial unless you know precisely what you are doing. Understand?" The operator always evoked a laugh. "Oh, I got her again. I got the grumpy lady."

The Comedy Museum was in operation for forty minutes. At the end of this time, the older and younger children gathered in a circle. Some of the fifth graders led a singdown of humorous camp songs. The seven- and eight-year-olds then had a chance to tell a joke, ask a riddle, or describe something that struck them as funny at the Comedy Museum. We ended by eating homemade "smile" cookies and pieces of Chuckles candy.

REFLECTIONS ON OUTCOMES

The fifth graders were exposed to a variety of humorous books and authors as they explored fiction, poetry, and biographies. They saw that they could cull information from nonprint materials as they made extensive use of records, audio- and videocassettes, and films. They used public libraries to obtain information about radio, early television, and silent films. They developed a humor and comedy vocabulary. They saw that comedy was hard work, as they tried things out and tested new material. They examined the roots of humor and how comedy reflects a society or culture, and they began to acquire a historical perspective about the subject. They saw the links between humor and pain, comedy and tragedy. They learned that many comics grew up in poverty and experienced painful childhoods. They developed an aesthetic appreciation of comedy as they learned classical routines, created their own humorous writings, and discussed why certain works seemed timeless.

Students drew upon inner resources as they worked out the problems of creating their comedy museum. They improved the teaching skills they had mastered as instructors at the Pirate Academy the previous year. They were more at ease as performers and communicators, and this helped them feel independent and accomplished.

The careful planning that went into choosing the pairs and small working groups yielded unexpected rewards. Students rarely wasted time fooling around; they collaborated quite well and concentrated on planning and creating their lessons. They were able to step into different roles because they had been removed from their usual social groups. In some cases, new friendships began to form. The comedy museum helped them to renew their sense of trust in themselves, and in one another. This served to counterbalance some of the rocky times they were having in the classroom. They also must have felt enormous security seeing their two teachers work together in a nurturing way and having such a terrific and playful time. Cynthia and I knew that neither of us would have initiated such an open-ended project with this volatile group by ourselves. Together we were able to combine our strengths, take the necessary risks, and succeed.

References

Books

Aardema, Verna. *What's So Funny, Ketu?* ill. by Marc Brown. Dial, 1982.
Adler, David A. *The Children of Chelm*, ill. by Arthur Friedman. Bonin, 1979.
Ahlberg, Janet, and Allan Ahlberg. *The Jolly Postman or Other People's Letters*. Little, 1986.
Andersen, Hans Christian. *The Emperor's New Clothes*, retold and ill. by Anne Rockwell. Harper, 1982.

Barrett, Judi. *Animals Should Definitely Not Wear Clothing,* ill. by Ron Barrett. Atheneum, 1980.

————. *Cloudy with a Chance of Meatballs,* ill. by Ron Barrett. Atheneum, 1978.

Belpré, Pura. *Perez and Martina; A Portorican Folk Tale,* ill. by Carlos Sanchez. Warne, 1961.

————. "The Wolf, the Fox, and Jug of Honey" in *The Tiger and the Rabbit and Other Tales,* ill. by Tomie dePaola. Lippincott, 1965.

Bird, E. J. *Ten Tall Tales.* Carolrhoda, 1984.

Clements, Bruce. *I Tell a Lie Every So Often.* Farrar, 1974.

Conford, Ellen. *Hail! Hail! Camp Timberwood.* Little, 1978.

Courlander, Harold, and George Herzog. "Talk" in *The Cow-Tail Switch and Other West African Stories.* Holt, 1947.

Danziger, Paula. *There's a Bat in Bunk Five.* Delacorte, 1980.

dePaola, Tomie. *Strega Nona: An Old Tale.* Prentice-Hall, 1975.

Dubanevich, Arlene. *Pigs in Hiding.* Four Winds, 1983.

Fleischman, Sid. *The Whipping Boy,* ill. by Peter Sis. Greenwillow, 1986.

Galdone, Joanna. *The Tailypo: A Ghost Story,* ill. by Paul Galdone. Seabury, 1977.

Galdone, Paul. *The Frog Prince.* McGraw-Hill, 1974.

————. *The Gingerbread Boy.* Seabury, 1975.

————. *The Little Red Hen.* Seabury, 1973.

Gerstein, Mordicai. *Tales of Pan.* Harper, 1986.

Henry, O. "The Ransom of Red Chief" in *Tales of O. Henry.* Doubleday, 1969.

Kellogg, Steven. *Pecos Bill.* Morrow, 1986.

Lester, Julius. "Why Dogs Hate Cats" in *The Knee-High Man and Other Tales,* ill. by Ralph Pinto. Dial 1972.

Lipsyte, Robert. *One Fat Summer.* Harper, 1977.

McCloskey, Robert. *Homer Price.* Viking, 1943.

Mahy, Margaret. *The Man Whose Mother Was a Pirate,* ill. by Margaret Chamberlain. Viking, 1985.

Noble, Trinka H. *The Day Jimmy's Boa Ate the Wash,* ill. by Steven Kellogg. Dial, 1980.

————. *Meanwhile Back at the Ranch,* ill. by Tony Ross. Dial, 1987.

Parish, Peggy. *Amelia Bedelia,* ill. by Fritz Siebel. Harper, 1963.

Park, Barbara. *Skinnybones.* Knopf, 1982.

Phelps, Ethel J., ed. "Three Strong Women" in *Tatterhood and Other Tales,* Feminist, 1978.

Pinkwater, Daniel Manus. *Fat Men from Space.* Dodd, 1977.

Prelutsky, Jack. *Nightmares: Poems to Trouble Your Sleep,* ill. by Arnold Lobel. Greenwillow, 1976.

————. *Rolling Harvey down the Hill,* ill. by Victoria Chess. Greenwillow, 1980.

Rey, H. A. *Curios George.* Houghton, 1941.

Sachs, Marilyn. *Dorrie's Book.* Doubleday, 1975.

Salinger, J. D. *Catcher in the Rye.* Little, 1951.

Schwartz, Alvin. *Unriddling: All Sorts of Riddles to Puzzle Your Guessery,* ill. by Sue Truesdell. Lippincott, 1983.

————. *Whoppers: Tall Tales and Other Lies,* ill. by Glen Rounds. Harper, 1975.

Selden, George. *The Dunkard,* ill. by Peter Lippman. Harper, 1968.

Sendak, Maurice. *Pierre: A Cautionary Tale in Five Chapters and a Prologue.* Harper, 1962.

Settel, Irving, and William Laas. *A Pictorial History of Television.* Grisset, 1967.
Seuling, Barbara. *The Teeny Tiny Woman: An Old English Ghost Tale.* Viking, 1976.
Seuss, Dr. *On Beyond Zebra.* Random, 1955.
————. *Yertle the Turtle, and Other Stories.* Random, 1958.
Singer, Isaac Bashevis. "Zlateh the Goat," in *Zlateh the Goat and Other Stories.* Harper, 1966.
Sobol, Donald J. *Encyclopedia Brown, Boy Detective.* Nelson, 1963.
Steig, William. *The Real Thief.* Farrar, 1973.
Stevenson, James. *Could Be Worse.* Greenwillow, 1977.
Tapio, Pat Decker. *The Lady Who Saw the Good Side to Everything,* ill. by Paul Galdone. Seabury, 1975.
Thurber, James. "The Night the Bed Fell" in *My Life and Hard Times.* Harper, 1933.
————. *The Secret Life of Walter Mitty.* Creative Ed., 1983.
Wiesner, William. *Turnabout: A Norwegian Tale.* Seabury, 1972.
Wouk, Herman. *City Boy: The Adventures of Herbie Bookbinder.* Doubleday, 1969.

Films

The Chicken. Pathe, 1965. 15 min.
Cooley High, dir. by Michael Schultz. American International, 1975. 107 min.
The Court Jester, dir. by Norman Panama and Melvin Frank. Paramount, 1956. 101 min.
Gerald McBoing-Boing. UPA, 1950. 8 min.
The Gold Rush, dir. by Charlie Chaplin. United Artists, 1925. 81 min.
Hope and Glory, dir. by John Boorman. Columbia, 1987. 112 min.
Madeline. UPA, 1952. 7 min.
Munro. Rembrant, 1960. 10 min.
People Soup. Learning Corporation of America, 1970. 12 min.
Pigbird. Canadian Film Board, 1983. 3 min.
Stalag 17, dir. by Billy Wilder. Paramount, 1953, 120 min.

Recordings and Songs

"Camp Granada" in *My Son, the Nut,* composed and performed by Allan Sherman (audio recording). Warner, 1963.
"A Very Merry Unbirthday" in *Walt Disney's Story of Alice in Wonderland* (audio recording). Disney, 1969.
"When I Was a Kid," written and performed by Bill Cosby (audio recording). Universal City Records, 1971.
"Who's on First?" in *Who's on First? Abbott and Costello on Radio!* (audio recording). Radiola, 1974.
"You've Got to Have Heart" in *Damn Yankees,* comp. by Jerold Rosenberg (audio recording). RCA, 1955.

The Third Journey:
Special Places and
Fantasy Worlds

Introduction to the Theme

Most childhood years are spent in coming to terms with the real world of home, family, school, and community. Children often develop and test their understanding of that world by constructing and entering private worlds of play and imagination. In these special places, they can recreate their home world in all its aspects. They can take risks, go on adventures, and get back safely when danger is lurking. Hideouts and forts allow children to be in control of their world, to create their own rules and rituals, and to express their special identity. Having a special or secret place to which they can retreat gives children a sense of privacy and a feeling of solitude. They can explore their fantasies and act out a variety of life's possible dramas.

Special places can be in caves, vacant lots, or the corners of a room. They can be simple or elaborate. They can involve one person, several people, or a group. They can be a source for contemplation, or for high-spirited adventuring. They can exist in the real world or in the imagination. Whatever their character, these places always matter immensely to the children who create them.

Urban children, in particular, often have to deal with crowded apartments, limited play spaces, and a constant barrage of noises and visual stimuli. These factors intensify their need to escape, to establish a separate, private world of their own, a world they can put into order and need not explain to anyone. A private spot can lend itself to a number of enriching activities: reading, storywriting, drawing, sketching, or playing an instrument.

Picture books such as *Evan's Corner* (Hill), *A Small Lot* (Keith), and *The Big Pile of Dirt* (Clymer) illustrate how finding, taking over, or organizing a special place can help children to individualize and define themselves. Decorating and transforming a hideout can help them feel a sense of power and know that they can shape and modify their environment even in modest ways.

Sometimes a special place has to do with associations made with a special person and a series of shared adventures. In *My Island Grandma* (Lasky) and *Grandaddy's*

Place (Griffith), children are allowed to enter delightful other worlds where they are nurtured and recognized, can feel expansive, and can express themselves fully. The creation of a secret world by two protagonists helps them support each other and build a powerful, intimate bond in *Bridge to Terabithia* (Paterson). A reindeer blanket and familiar beloved objects provide a young Innuit boy with feelings of coziness and infinite security in *On Mother's Lap* (Scott). Occasionally, these special places can become threatened and endangered, and children must either fight to protect their worlds or anticipate and accept the fact of losing them. Such dilemmas occur in *Miguel's Mountain* (Binzen) and *Adam's Common* (Wiseman); threats are resolved courageously and resourcefully in both stories.

When children are involved with their friends in having a secret place or clubhouse, they learn to share, make decisions, and compromise without grownups acting to supervise or interfere. These can be imaginative and adventurous times, as club members spy on others from lookout points and communicate with passwords, codes, and secret knocks, as in the film *Stand by Me* (Reiner).

A secret place can be a refuge from fear and desperation. In this other place, a child or young adult can separate from intense family dynamics or escape from being picked on or abused. He or she can feel some temporary easing of whatever harshness is encountered at home. The title character in *Slake's Limbo* (Holman) seeks to survive in the New York subway system, but this experience also compounds his sense of isolation.

Extraordinary secret worlds abound in children's literature. Through the process of reading, children can be transported to the fantasy lands of Oz, Never Never Land, Narnia, Middle Earth, Dictionopolis, the Mushroom Planet, or Tom's Midnight Garden. Children may want to consider these questions: Why do only certain individuals discover and enter these fantasy places? Do these characters have any qualities in common? How are they changed by the journeys they make, and how do the characters affect those whom they meet?

Using knights and castles, dolls and dollhouses, or simple cloth puppets and makeshift stages, children can derive endless joy from owning a kingdom and creating its language and laws through dramatic play. These small theatrical arenas stimulate children to become authors and storytellers as they bring their characters to life and set up interactions and story lines.

Routes

Beginning the Journey

WITH YOUNGER CHILDREN (PRE-K–GRADE 2)

The library media specialist could start the journey by reading aloud *Six Special Places* (De Bruyn), a humorous account of three children's efforts to make a hideout and the problems they encounter (natural elements, annoyed parents, outside intruders). Children then discuss the special or secret places they have enjoyed. "How and where did you discover your special place? Who else knew about it? How long did you have it? How would you describe it? What adventures did you have there? Did you have a secret language or code?"

During a second session, students work in pairs designing their ideal hideouts on large pieces of posterboard. They could develop a set of drawings showing the inside view, the outside view, the surrounding area, nearby points of interest (a creek, wishing well, nest), and any special features of the hideout (wind chimes, pulleys).

WITH MIDDLE GRADE CHILDREN (GRADES 3–5)

The library media specialist could read the first passages of *Harriet the Spy* (Fitzhugh), in which Harriet explains to her friend how to play "Town" by making up the name, then writing down the names of all the inhabitants (she recommends about twenty-five, "or it gets too hard"). After some discussion about this novel, the group could choose a name for an imaginary town and then create life-sized cardboard figures of adults who reside there. These figures could be quite humorous, perhaps in the cartoon style of *Red Grooms' Ruckus Rodeo* (Haskell).

Children then document the lives and histories of their imaginary cardboard characters through the making of fictitious scrapbooks. They could use actual or devised baby photos, report cards, letters written and received, invitations, newspaper articles, family emblems, passports, and wedding announcements. For example, I. M. Noisy's scrapbook contains a set of illustrated noise cards that he invented. Similar to flash cards, they show the instruments that make sounds: a bullhorn, mouth, microphone, and megaphone. There is also a letter of advice written to I. M.'s mother:

Dear Mrs. Noisy,

Your son's problem is merely just the worst case of Noisy disease. The only way to cure it is to tell your son to talk with his mouth closed.

Sincerely, Dr. Joyce Sisters (Timothy Gilliam, age 10)

WITH OLDER CHILDREN (GRADES 6-UP)

The library media specialist reads aloud *Bored—Nothing to Do* (Spier), which describes how two boys build an airplane after scavenging materials from around the house. Another possibility would be *Regards to the Man in the Moon* (Keats).

The class is divided into groups of three or four. Each group is given a bag of junk, and is asked to create a world with the junk, and a story that takes place in that world. The junk might include anything: a battery, key, acorn, straw, mirror, tube, piece of driftwood, spool, compass, pinecone, watch part, fabric, ribbon, jewel, clothespin, cork, button.

After a period of twenty minutes or so, the class travels from area to area, visiting the various junk worlds and listening to the stories or story beginnings. Each group could also share their starting point, the object or objects that sparked the building of that world. A funnel, used as a pyramid, might be the keystone object in the creating of an Egyptian environment.

When children create "junk worlds," they often make mythical settings and adventure stories involving quests and magical elements. Some groups create futuristic worlds. Some create the world of knights, or worlds under the sea. Some groups have created everyday worlds like circuses, farms, hospitals, and parks. This is a very stimulating and collaborative activity that encourages verbalization and can be effective with all age groups. Most often the results are quite remarkable, and children may insist that their worlds be kept on display for a time (see fig. 9).

Excursions

VERBAL

"Nursery Rhyme Secrets." Younger children create little plays about the secrets and secret places of various nursery rhyme characters. Jack and Jill might have a secret fort on the top of the hill. Humpty Dumpty might be sitting on the king's royal jokebook. Jack Be Nimble might know a secret way to get into the candle factory.

"Fantasy Land Encounters." Working in pairs, middle grade students dramatize some of the first encounters that occur when particular literary characters enter their fantasy lands. What are their concerns at the time? What are their first impressions? What are they thinking and feeling during these encounters? Are the characters they meet kind, evil, humorous, magical? Some possibilities: Alice's fall down the rabbit hole and encounter with the White Rabbit; Dorothy's encounter with the Munchkins in Oz; Gulliver's encounter with the Lilliputians.

"Clubhouse Dramas." Middle grade and older students develop dramatizations about incidents happening in a clubhouse, fort, or secret place. Some possibilities: a new person wants to join the club; a conflict occurs about making a decision; someone mysterious leaves special gifts in the hideout; a neighbor accuses the club members of being vandals; club members adopt an unusual club mascot.

WRITTEN

"The Fairy Tale Lecture Series." Residents of the fairy tale kingdom write speeches or lectures demonstrating their particular talents or skills. Cinderella's Fairy Godmother might describe fifty things one can make with a pumpkin. Pin-

Special Places and Fantasy Worlds: Other Ways to Begin	Stories to Tell	Works to Read Aloud	Films to Share
Younger grades Pre-K–2nd	"The Princess and the Pea" (Andersen)	*Through the Magic Mirror* (Browne)	*Where the Wild Things Are*
	The Inch Boy (Morimoto)	*When the Forest Meets the Sea* (Baker)	*The Sand Castle*
	My Father's Dragon (Gannett)	*The Most Beautiful Place in the World* (Cameron)	*Santiago's Ark*
Middle grades 3rd–5th	*Fog Magic* (Sauer)	*How I Hunted the Little Fellows* (Zhitkov)	*Calder's Circus*
	The Fisherman and His Wife (Grimm)	*A Man Named Thoreau* (Burleigh)	*Castle*
	Alice's Adventures in Wonderland (Carroll)	*The Animal Family* (Jarrell)	*The Phantom Tollbooth*
Upper grades 6th–8th	"The Crab Prince" (Calvino)	*Below the Root* (Snyder)	*He Makes Me Feel like Dancin'*
	Journey Outside (Steele)	*A Wizard of Earthsea* (Le Guin)	*The Circus*
	The Secret Life of Walter Mitty (Thurber)	*The Planet of Junior Brown* (Hamilton)	*Yellow Submarine*

Fig. 9. Special Places and Fantasy Worlds: Other Ways to Begin

occhio might give a lecture on the art of telling the truth. The Second Little Pig might lead a seminar on housing problems. The Giant could provide tips on catching a Jack:

> The most important thing is to use your nose because Jack has this strange smell about him of licorice and pumpkin pie. If you smell those smells, get your silverware ready. Now I will teach you what a giant says when he smells a Jack. (Michael Reynolds, age 10)

> A servant in the castle describes how to make the Queen whine. "The first step is to tell her there is a piece of cherry tart stuck on her royal throne. If that doesn't work, tell her that her royal tea came from an old peasant's recipe. She'll probably spill it out in the royal trashcan. If that doesn't work, tell her that one of her royal lemons is sour." (John Fraidstern, age10)

"Character Writings." Children write poems as though they were a character from a fantasy world based on their sense of that character. They would need to know how characters feel about themselves and their world—about their dreams, wishes, fears, passions, secrets and concerns. For example, after listening to *The Wind in the Willows* (Grahame), some students created poems and other writings as if they were the character Mole:

> Some things that remind me about spring are wind and trees, and a cool spring breeze. These are some things that remind me about summer: the sun, a pond, and I am very fond of a boat ride. (Michael Quattrone, age 9)

> Hi. I'm Mr. Mole. I live underground. I do spring cleaning in the spring. My friend Toad is rich, conceited and a bad driver. He gets himself into a lot of trouble. Once he was even put in jail. (Zoey Johnson, age 10)

"Folk Tale Magazines." Children in pairs create magazine issues that describe the news and activities of the fairy tale kingdom. At first they could examine a variety of familiar periodicals such as *Cricket, Faces, Ranger Rick,* or *Time,* and make a list of some of the typical features and sections—editorials, interviews, fashions, sports, weather reports, book reviews, funnies, want ads, advice columns, and so on. Time should be spent studying how to make up effective headlines and how to write lively news stories. A magazine issue could feature an interview with Bear family members after they return home from their walk. ("I just couldn't believe it. The porridge was gone. The chairs were broken.") A sports story might capture Jack's record-breaking climb down the beanstalk. Nine- and ten-year-olds produced a magazine called *Rumplestiltsin Today* (see fig. 10).

ART AND MUSIC

"Fantasy Board Games." Children create board games involving characters from familiar nursery rhymes, fairy tales, or fantasy books. These characters

Fig. 10. An Issue of *Rumplestiltsin* [sic] *Today*. Used with permission

have a definite goal or quest (Dorothy tries to get back home to Kansas, Frodo searches for the magic ring). The games might feature cards like "chance" or "community chest", as in *Monopoly;* advantages and shortcuts; penalties and obstacles; rewards; a safety zone; dice or a spinner. In a *Jack and the Beanstalk* board game, for example, if a player falls into the Giant's soup, she has to go back home and dry off. If she lands on the Giant's harp, she forfeits her turn to play a tune. If she steals the Golden Goose, she can go ahead seven spaces.

"Travel Brochures." Individually or in pairs, students create travel brochures of various fantasy lands that would attract potential tourists. They should include information about characters they might meet there, possible thrills and adventures, facilities, bargains, group rates. "Come to Oz. Follow the Yellow Brick Road. Throw water on the Wicked Witch of the West. Shop at the Emerald City. Learn about courage from the Cowardly Lion."

"Entrances to Fantasy Lands." Students identify and describe the kinds of entrances (mirror, wardrobe, looking glass, rabbit hole, tollbooth) authors have created to their various imaginary lands. "How do people get transported to these special worlds? Do each of these entrances have a distinctive look?" After talking about a few, the library media specialist could divide the class into small groups. Each group could choose an entrance, design it through drawings and, if possible, sculpt it through wire and papier-mâché.

"The Never Never Land Choir." Students listen to any one of several delightful, well-known film scores based on classic stories, learn some of the songs that describe special places, and perform them as members of a choir. Some possibilities might be "Under the Sea" from *The Little Mermaid;* "Over the Rainbow" from *The Wizard of Oz;* and "Never Never Land" from *Peter Pan.* Children may want to adapt other works into musicals, creating original songs for such stories as *The Swineherd* (Andersen) or *White Wave* (Wolkstein).

RESEARCH

"Favorite Places Poll." Younger children could develop a questionnaire, and interview one or two of the important grownups in their lives to learn about their special childhood places. The results could be shared in a discussion, and a large list of places could be made and displayed with photos and drawings.

"Fantasy Authors." Middle grade and older students might be fascinated researching the early lives of their favorite fantasy-book authors. What games did they play? What toys or treasures did they value? When were they first involved creating stories and plays? Who influenced them? Who nurtured and recognized their talents? What books did they love? Were they always obsessed with fantasy worlds? When did they experience pain and rejection? In Roald Dahl's *Boy,* you can trace the roots of *Charlie and the Chocolate Factory* when the author describes deliciously his visits to the candy shop and his discovery of gob-stoppers.

"Folk Tale Derivatives." Students investigate versions of their favorite folk-tales that exist in other cultures. They could then share their findings through a panel or story presentation. Someone might tell the popular Perrault version of *Cinderella*. Another student might tell or read aloud the English version, *Tattercoats* (Steel). Others might share *Nomi and the Magic Fish* (M'Bane), an African derivation, or perhaps *Yeh-Shen: A Cinderella Story from China* (Louie). They could then point out the differences in character and plot development, perhaps in the styles of illustration as well.

"Film Fantasy Worlds." Children research the design of fantasy worlds in animated and live-action films. What processes and special effects are used? How many artists are employed? How long does their labor take? How did Walt Disney create Bald Mountain in *Fantasia,* and what went into the creation of Jim Henson's *The Dark Crystal* ? Students could check *The Art of Walt Disney: From Mickey Mouse to the Magic Kingdoms* (Finch) and *The Making of the Dark Crystal: Creating a Unique Film* (Finch). Students might want to create a display with models, sketches, and demonstrations of techniques.

Celebrations

"Mother Goose March." Younger kids create a parade of the homes of nursery rhyme characters that would travel to a senior center. Children could make simple costumes and use wagons for constructing floats. They might want to present songs, pantomimes, and souvenir boxes containing Little Bo Peep ribbons and staffs and Little Boy Blue paper horns. The children could then serve their audience samples of Humpty Dumpty egg salad.

"The Pocket-Sized Universe." Children could create an exhibit of miniature environments. These might include button gardens and matchbox worlds. A demonstration of miniature bowling could involve visitors in using marbles to knock down wooden golf tees.

"Fantasy Kite Day." Divided into small groups, children choose a fantasy book and then design and build a kite that would symbolize their book. An Oz group, for example, might fashion their kite from red and green paper or cloth to represent the ruby slippers and the Emerald City. The celebration day would involve children displaying and flying their kites in a playground or park.

"County Fair." Children create a county fair in honor of the characters in *Charlotte's Web* (White). Some children could transform the schoolyard into a fairground with bales of hay and cutout calico pigs. Other children, operating the general store, could sell penny bags of seeds and homemade farmer's almanacs. There could be miniature scarecrow-making and barn-raising events, an arcade of country games (marbles, horseshoes), and even a one-room schoolhouse.

"The Camelot Institute." Using the format of the Pirate Academy, older children develop special schools to prepare younger kids for knighthood. At Heralding School, they could teach them how to announce both good news and bad news. They could develop curricula for Squire School, Good Deeds School, Fair Maiden School, and Chivalry School. Some children might attend a fancy printing school conducted by one of Guenevere's scribes. Merlin, as school guidance counselor, could give his advice about the future in a special assembly. The festivities might include a tournament and banquet. The day would culminate when King Arthur knights each youngster with Excalibur, and then reads aloud from *The Sword in the Stone* (White). Someone else might tell or read *Ruby, the Red Knight* (Aitken).

A Journey Log: The "Wee People Curriculum"

The cubby people live in Miss Green's third grade classroom in the empty cubby. The class doesn't know anything about them. They try to keep the secret by doing all the errands at recess or at night. The cubby children have little desks made out of cardboard. They use broken tips of lead from pencils so they can learn right along with the class. (Lisa Koulish, age 8)

STEP ONE: CHOOSING THE THEME

I developed the "wee people curriculum" specifically for a class of seven- and eight-year-olds. I wanted to reinforce the idea that the library was a story place where, sometimes, they could be storymakers as well as story readers, becoming authors and making their own library books; they were so enthusiastic about their newly acquired reading skills. Emily, their teacher, had also been working hard with them on developing writing skills. She felt that they were ready for the challenge of creating their own books about tiny people. In doing so, the children could feel like giants themselves. These sevens/eights entered projects with ebullience and imagination. They loved to experiment and could now handle the longer, more sustained effort the "wee people" unit would demand from them.

STEP TWO: PLANNING THE JOURNEY

The bulk of the planning was done with sixth grade library assistants who enjoyed sharing some favorite books from earlier years, and then reviewed some more recent works. Two of the assistants designed and constructed over twenty blank books for the project. A third one suggested the idea of having a banquet. The head teacher, Emily, was quite supportive of this venture, and we were able to confer several times as the journey progressed. The emphasis in the classroom was more on expository writing and the description of everyday feelings and occurrences. This kind of imaginative writing was different; children were encouraged to be wild and fanciful in the creation of stories. She was struck by her students' enthusiasm for the wee books they were making. In our feedback sessions she and I discovered we were learning a good deal about the special qualities and interests of individual children.

STEP THREE: BEGINNING THE JOURNEY

In the first session, I gave the seven- and eight-year-olds a nonsense test about folktale and fantasy book characters, just to get them thinking about these particular realms. I administered the test with utter seriousness, stressing how important it was to be an "earnest and righteous" test taker. Quite soon, they were chuckling and chortling, trying hard not to lose control (see fig. 11).

1. Cinderella's Fairy Godmother was able to transform a pumpkin into
   A. a ten-speed bike   C. a golden coach
   B. a skate board   D. a Volkswagon

2. Whenever Pinocchio lied,
   A. he sneezed   C. his nose grew
   B. his ears twitched   D. he hiccupped

3. The First Little Pig built his house out of
   A. tinker toys   C. toothpicks
   B. silly putty   D. straw

4. The young hero Jack traded his cow for
   A. a flashlight   C. a bongo drum
   B. some baseball cards   D. some beans

5. The Troll waited for the Three Billy Goats by the
   A. bowling alley   C. bridge
   B. video store   D. mall

6. Dorothy grew homesick as she thought about her home
   A. in Tanzania   C. in Rhode Island
   B. in Miami Beach   D. in Kansas

7. Captain Hook enjoyed his work as a
   A. pirate   C. receptionist
   B. guidance counselor   D. dentist

8. The Wicked Queen tried to trick Snow White with
   A. some yogurt   C. a tuna on rye
   B. a meatball hero   D. an apple

Fig. 11. The International Folk Tale Exam

Afterwards, we discussed what the characters in the test shared in common, and students quickly discerned that they all lived in or visited some kind of "make-believe" world. I then showed them how and where in the library they could find folktales and fantasy books. We spent the remainder of the time browsing and reading these books to one another, and rediscovering some old friends.

STEP FOUR: TAKING SOME EXCURSIONS

In the second session, I read *Mrs. Vinegar* (Stern), about a wee person who, with her husband, must search for a new home when their bottle house is broken during spring cleaning. I then asked the group to think of any of the tiny people who existed in children's books. They listed the following characters and types: the Borrowers, the Littles, Tom Thumb, Tinker Bell, Thumbelina, elves, fairies, leprechauns, trolls. I asked what advantages there might be if one were to become a wee person. The children were intrigued by this and many of them felt that being a tiny person would allow easy access to many kinds of places. "You could sneak into places. You could get into movies and baseball games for free." Some liked the idea of perhaps having magic powers if they were elves or fairies. Disadvantages, they concluded, would be any encounters you might have with dogs, cats, rats, roaches, and spiders. When asked if anyone would like to be a wee person for at least a day, most students resoundingly said "Yes!" They seemed very enthusiastic about this theme. It appealed to their delight in knowing secrets and having secret powers.

In the third session, I read *The Tomten* (Lindgren), about a protective troll who watches over a Swedish farm, and *Quimble Wood* (Bodecker), a delightful survival story about a miniature world. I then asked them to imagine that they were seashell people, living in a conch in a safe place near the sea. I showed them what a conch looked like, and how you could hear the whispering of the sea if you held it to your ear. I asked them how they could use the resources and natural materials of the beach for their survival. (A crab leg could be a digging tool, a sea gull feather could be used for sweeping, a piece of driftwood could become furniture, seaweed might serve as salad greens.) I then asked them what might be scary situations for seashell people (high tides, heavy rains, lobsters).

I introduced them to the idea of creating their own books about imaginary wee people. We talked about the content of the books, what they might include that would "explain" about their people: physical descriptions, habits, problems, struggles, maps of their environment, legends and poems, fashions, games, jokes, riddles, sayings, kinds of dwellings, celebrations.

We then explored some of the possibilities for settings: a piccolo, drum, bakery, pencil sharpener, nest, pool table, cloud. I told them to decide by the next session where they wanted their wee people to live and whether they wanted to work individually or with a partner.

During the next three sessions, the sevens/eights seemed quite involved in their writing and drawing. Most of them worked in pairs, but there were a few students who preferred to work alone. At the end of the sixth session, I taught the group "Inchworm" and "Thumbelina," two songs from the film *Hans Christian Andersen* (Vidor). Then I invited them to attend the Wee People's Banquet to be held the following week. During this special celebration, I explained, they would at last be able to share their books with each other.

STEP FIVE: CELEBRATING THE JOURNEY

The sevens/eights head teacher, assistant teacher, four of my sixth grade assistants, and a visiting friend helped me to plan and prepare the Wee People's Banquet. The sixth graders made placemats with drawings of elves and fairies. They also transformed the library with decorations and created a child-sized, papier-mâché rabbit hole.

On the day of celebration, the seven- and eight-year-olds were led to an empty classroom that they entered by crawling through the rabbit hole. This, of course, aroused their curiosity. A collection of books featuring wee people was displayed on one of the tables.

Quietly, we formed a circle and began our ceremony by singing "Inchworm" and "Thumbelina." Each person then shared his or her book, describing where the wee people lived, what they looked like, and what their habits and interests were.

> The people of the mousehole family are very friendly, and they are very poor. That's why they dig in the garbage. And they are not so healthy, but they live through it. (Lauren Weiss, age 8)

> The tree fairies listen to Mozart. Their enemies are the lightning bugs. Their habits are biting their nails and collecting beachnuts. Once a year they gather around their tree and eat pears. (Annie Egelson, age 8)

> The armor people live in a suit of armor at the museum. They are sometimes war-like and sometimes peaceful. Their poem reads "A knight is bright when he has to fight." The armor people wear three kinds of fashions: knightwear, partywear, and sleepwear. (Lucas Nivon, age 8 and Gaby Giordani, age 9)

> The Beams live in the eleventh light in the town library. Their neighbors, the Shines, live in the third light. Now it happened to be Lightmas, and Mrs. Beam was busy making her famous light cake. She bustled about making page pudding and cover cupcakes. She made light lemonade and glow teas for the beverages. Then the Shines came as always, and they all stood for the Lightmas poem. (Sarah Tucker, age 9)

After the ceremony, we led the sevens/eights to the library to begin the Wee People's Banquet. The children looked surprised and subdued as they glimpsed the long table. There were twenty illustrated placemats, twenty medicine cups, and twenty tiny bowls. Each bowl contained one gumdrop, one peanut, one chocolate kiss, one animal cracker, two raisins, and three sunflower seeds.

We all raised our tiny cups of fruit punch and took turns around the table, toasting some of the tiny important things of life. We toasted jacks, bells, marbles, thimbles, arrowheads, walnut shells, hummingbird eggs, acorns, rice krispies, cheerios, amoebas, ladybugs, pennies, and dimes. We must have refilled those medicine cups at least ten or eleven times. "Eat slowly," Emily, the head teacher, suggested. "Wee people always eat slowly." Then there was one more round of toasting as we paid tribute to Tinker Bell, Tom Thumb, all of the Borrowers, and all of the Littles.

REFLECTIONS ON OUTCOMES

This curriculum involved children in listening to stories, reading stories, and writing their own stories. They were introduced to the genres of folktales and fantasy books and to some of the important fantasy book authors. They learned where in the library they could find these books.

They created an imaginary culture and had to think about many of its dimensions. In trying to solve problems, they combined fantasy with logic, employing both creative and critical thinking skills. How would their wee people take care of themselves? How would they use the natural resources of their surroundings?

Most children were involved in partnerships and had to work out the fair division of labor to bring their project to completion. All of the children learned to enjoy their role as authors, sharing their works with peers and teachers at the "Wee People" ceremony, and, later, with younger children during a rest period. These authors were able to feel grown up and to engage in grown-up rituals— attending a banquet and making toasts. They began to know the library as a place for joining with others in the creation of secret worlds and story surprises.

References

Books

Aitken, Amy. *Ruby, the Red Knight.* Bradbury, 1983.
Andersen, Hans Christian. "The Princess and the Pea" in *It's Perfectly True, and Other Stories,* ill. by Richard Bennett. Harcourt, 1938.
———. *The Swineherd,* ill. by Lisbeth Zwerger. Morrow, 1982.
Baker, Jeannie. *When the Forest Meets the Sea.* Greenwillow, 1987.
Binzen, Bill. *Miguel's Mountain.* Coward, 1968.
Bodecker, N. M. *Quimble Wood,* ill. by Branka Starr. Atheneum, 1981.
Browne, Anthony. *Through the Magic Mirror.* Greenwillow, 1977.
Burleigh, Robert. *A Man Named Thoreau,* ill. by Lloyd Bloom. Atheneum, 1985.
Calvino, Italo. "The Crab Prince" in *Italian Folk Tales.* Harcourt, 1980.
Cameron, Ann. *The Most Beautiful Place in the World.* Knopf, 1988.

Carroll, Lewis. *Alice's Adventures in Wonderland,* ill. by Sir John Tenniel. St. Martin's, 1977.

Clymer, Eleanor. *The Big Pile of Dirt,* ill. by Robert Shore. Holt, 1968.

Dahl, Roald. *Boy: Tales of Childhood.* Farrar, 1984.

———. *Charlie and the Chocolate Factory.* Knopf, 1964.

De Bruyn, Monica. *Six Special Places.* Whitman, 1975.

Finch, Christopher. *The Art of Walt Disney: From Mickey Mouse to the Magic Kingdoms.* Abrams, 1973.

———. *The Making of The Dark Crystal: Creating a Unique Film.* Abrams, 1975.

Fitzhugh, Louise. *Harriet the Spy.* Harper, 1964.

Gannett, Ruth S. *My Father's Dragon.* Random, 1948.

Grahame, Kenneth. *The Wind in the Willows.* Scribners, 1933.

Griffith, Helen V. *Grandaddy's Place,* ill. by James Stevenson. Greenwillow, 1987.

Grimm, Jacob, and Wilhelm K. Grimm. *The Fisherman and His Wife,* trans. by Randall Jarrell and ill. by Margot Zemach. Farrar, 1980.

Hamilton, Virginia. *The Planet of Junior Brown.* Macmillan, 1971.

Haskell, Barbara. *Red Grooms' Ruckus Rodeo.* Abrams, 1988.

Hill, Elizabeth Starr. *Evan's Corner,* ill. by Nancy Grossman. Holt, 1967.

Holman, Felice. *Slake's Limbo.* Scribners, 1974.

Jarrell, Randall. *The Animal Family,* ill. by Maurice Sendak. Pantheon, 1965.

Keats, Ezra Jack. *Regards to the Man in the Moon.* Four Winds, 1981.

Keith, Eros. *A Small Lot.* Bradbury, 1968.

Lasky, Kathryn. *My Island Grandma.* Warne, 1979.

Le Guin, Ursula K. *A Wizard of Earthsea.* Houghton, 1968.

Lindgren, Astrid. *The Tomten,* ill. by Harald Wiberg. Coward, 1961.

Louie Ai-Ling. *Yeh-Shen: A Cinderella Story from China,* ill. by Ed Young. Philomel, 1982.

M'Bane, Phumla. *Nomi and the Magic Fish: A Story from Africa,* ill. by Carole Byard. Doubleday, 1972.

Morimoto, Junko. *The Inch Boy.* Viking, 1986.

Paterson, Katherine. *Bridge to Terebithia.* Crowell, 1977.

Perrault, Charles. *Cinderella: Or, the Little Glass Slipper,* ill. by Marcia Brown. Scribners, 1954.

Sauer, Julia. *Fog Magic.* Viking, 1943.

Scott, Ann Herbert. *On Mother's Lap,* ill. by Glo Coalson. McGraw, 1972.

Snyder, Zilpha. *Below the Root.* Atheneum, 1975.

Spier, Peter. *Bored—Nothing to Do.* Doubleday, 1978.

Steel, Flora Annie Webster. *Tattercoats: An Old English Tale,* ill. by Diane Goode. Bradbury, 1976.

Steele, Mary Q. *Journey Outside.* Viking, 1969.

Stern, Simon. *Mrs. Vinegar.* Prentice, 1979.

Thurber, James. *The Secret Life of Walter Mitty.* Creative Education, 1983.

White, E. B. *Charlotte's Web,* ill. by Garth Williams. Harper, 1952.

White, T. H. *The Sword in the Stone.* Putnam, 1939.

Wiseman, David. *Adam's Corner.* Houghton, 1984.

Wolkstein, Diane. *White Wave: A Chinese Tale,* ill. by Ed Young. Crowell, 1979.

Zhitkov, Boris. *How I Hunted the Little Fellows,* ill. by Paul O. Zelinsky. Dodd, 1979.

Films

Calder's Circus. McGraw-Hill. 1963. 20 min.

Castle. Unicorn, 1983. 58 min.

The Circus, dir. by Charlie Chaplin. United Artists, 1928. 72 min.

The Dark Crystal, dir. by Jim Henson and Frank Oz. Universal, 1982. 93 min.

Fantasia, dir. by Walt Disney. RKO, 1940. 135 min.

Hans Christian Andersen, dir. by Charles Vidor. Goldwyn, RKO Radio, 1952. 120 min.

He Makes Me Feel like Dancin'. Direct Cinema, 1984. 51 min.

The Phantom Tollbooth. MGM, 1970. 89 min.

The Sand Castle. Canadian Film Board, 1977. 13 min.

Santiago's Ark. ABC, 1973. 47 min.

Stand by Me, dir. by Rob Reiner. Columbia, 1986. 87 min.

Where the Wild Things Are. Weston Woods, 1973. 8 min.

Yellow Submarine, dir. by George Dunning. Britian, 1965. 85 min.

Recordings and Songs

"Inchworm" in *Song Hits from Hans Christian Andersen.* Words and music by Frank Loesser (audio recording). RCA, 1952.

"Never Never Land" in *Peter Pan,* composed by M. Charlap and performed by Mary Martin and original cast. RCA, 1954.

"Over the Rainbow" in *The Wizard of Oz.* Selections from original soundtrack. Words and music by E. Y. Harburg and H. Arlen (audio recording). MGM, 1956.

"Thumbelina" in *Song Hits from Hans Christian Andersen.* Words and music by Frank Loesser (audio recording). RCA, 1952.

"Under the Sea" in *The Little Mermaid.* Words and music by Howard Ashman and Alan Menkin (audio recording). Disney, 1989.

The Fourth Journey: Survival

Introduction to the Theme

Children must have their basic needs of food, clothing, and shelter satisfied. They must feel safe and nurtured in their home and family setting so that they can go out into the world with a sense of confidence. The concept of survival suggests a level of physical existence, in which basic human needs have been threatened, but then have been sustained or restored. Survival also suggests a deeper level of psychological existence in which emotional and cognitive needs are challenged by destructive forces or debilitating changes. To survive, one has to have faced significant losses, threats, dangers, or fears of annihilation. Children often experience such losses in relation to changes in their environment, changes in their relationships, and changes in themselves. Feelings of loss are sometimes based on anxiety. Some are based on reality. Many children have to deal with sickness or hospitalization, moving to a new neighborhood or community, or the crisis of a separation or divorce. Reality changes, often abruptly, and there are many feelings to sort out. But the pervasive question is, "What about me? Will I be hurt? Will I be safe?"

What does it mean for children to be uprooted, to be cut off from what is familiar and secure, to leave friends, routines, a particular landscape, a special hiding place? What does it mean for them emotionally to leave the place of their history? What are the feelings they carry inside? Fear? Confusion? Ambivalence? Hope? Despair?

If the emotional pain in children becomes acute, their need to escape escalates and deepens. Daydreaming can help ease this pain, and even provide a measure of hope. The artistic Donald in *Wingman* (Pinkwater) is a poignant character, teetering and insecure, very much on the edge of things. As the only Chinese kid in his school, he is exposed to racial slurs from both children and insensitive adults. This situation, coupled with the poverty of his home life, propels him to retreat into the safe, solitary world of comic-book heroes.

103

What sustains children when their lives are disrupted by extraordinary change? What are their memories, secrets, and dreams? What treasures and material things do they bring with them to deal with the transition? Will the harshness they encounter rob them of the chance to be playful? How will they express their humor? How will they interpret their situation and make sense of everything?

What happens to children caught up in the severity of wartime? How will they adapt and surive? The title character in *Petros' War* (Zei) is a ten-year-old Greek boy living in Athens during the German Occupation. His imagination helps him cope when the food is scarce and the mood is bleak. In his secret garden, with his turtle and beetles, he can dream and fantasize. His images of wearing armor and riding horses often help to nourish him and preserve his spirit.

In *Journey to Topaz* (Uchida), eleven-year-old Yuki is a Japanese-American who has just arrived at an evacuation camp in the Utah desert. In this new place, there is no vegetation, no trees or flowers. There are only ugly barracks and dust storms. Yet there is beauty even in this desolate world, and Yuki has the sensitivity to respond with awe and joy.

How do families in all times survive when they must constantly deal with poverty, hunger, and racism? What mechanisms and strengths help them to cope with day-to-day existing? How can music and stories help to ease their struggling and suffering? The young heroine of *Where the Lilies Bloom* (Cleaver) must hold her family together economically and emotionally and conceal her father's death from the authorities. *Roosevelt Grady* (Shotwell) depicts the migrant experience and the problems of even learning basic math when someone is always moving from school to school. *A Hero Ain't Nothin' but a Sandwich* (Childress) portrays a family ravaged by the destructiveness of drugs. Ester Wier's *The Loner* illustrates the compelling coming-of-age tale where the protagonist must cope courageously with unsettling changes.

How do cultures survive and preserve their uniqueness, their traditions, and arts? How can they coexist with the mainstream society, and not be forced to conform? How do minority groups, such as the Amish or Mexican-Americans, combat the acts of prejudice directed against them? What happens when a culture faces the possibility of annihilation, as did the Native Americans?

How do individuals and groups survive in the natural world? What are some of the skills that equip them to deal with rough and dangerous terrains? How could knowledge of the land and its resources be vital to someone? What are the ways one could forage for food or find water? How could one find protection during severe weather extremes? How could tools be devised from natural materials? *My Side of the Mountain* (George) and *Walkabout* (Marshall) depict journeys in which children learn to harmonize with nature and become competent and resourceful.

How can the environment survive when it is being neglected and polluted? How can concerned individuals organize, take action, educate others, and help create effective conservation laws? How can animals be protected? Which species are now in jeopardy? What animals have become extinct in the last ten years? What is the "greenhouse effect?" How do governments deal with nuclear waste? What damaging things to Earth's resources can never be changed?

Routes

Beginning the Journey

WITH YOUNGER CHILDREN (PRE-K–GRADE 2)

After the library media specialist reads *Swimmy* (Lionni), children discuss the various ways that animals protect themselves. Which animals use camouflage? Which animals have hard shells, powerful beaks, and claws? Which animals are swift, are expert tree climbers? Which animals are known for their intelligence? How do human beings survive? What are their strengths?

Each child then chooses a desert, farm, forest, jungle, or sea animal and finds information on how that animal protects itself and who its enemies are. Children then cut out photos or make simple drawings to illustrate their findings. The library media specialist develops a guessing game in which kids try to identify the secret animal.

WITH MIDDLE GRADE CHILDREN (GRADES 3–5)

The library media specialist could tell the Native American legend of *The Fire Bringer* (Hodges), which explains how a boy and coyote brought fire to the boy's tribe, and how this gift allowed the tribe to endure the cruel, chilling winter. Children could explore the friendship and trust that grew between the boy and coyote. How do they depend on each other? Do they really talk together, or can they just sense what the other is feeling? What can people learn from observing and knowing animals? What secrets could they reveal? Children develop this idea in writing, and then may choose to illustrate their work with paintings or develop their ideas into little plays or puppet shows.

"If you make friends with the red fox, he will lead you to food." (Deron Brown, age 8)

"A turtle climbs up a hill to speak to God and God tells him secrets and the turtle keeps the secrets under his shell." (Jason Arroyo, age 8)

WITH OLDER CHILDREN (GRADES 6-UP)

After reading aloud parts of *My Side of the Mountain* (George), the library media specialist asks students to write about the qualities and strengths that they possess that might help them survive in difficult situations:

My legs are strong. I don't get tired very easily, and I am bright. (Ricky Castillo, age 11)

If I had to survive, I would use my slyness, my courage and my brain. With all these things, I would probably survive. (Megan June, age 11)

I'm funny, creative, smart, good with my hands. I run fast, and most of all, I can speak a different language. (Katya Fiaklkova, age 11)

I can survive if I ever had to. I can work with my hands. I can talk a lot, and yell very loud. I know a lot about the world. And I'm intelligent. (Adjowah Scott, age 10)

Children could develop a list of specific pioneering skills that could help someone to survive alone in the woods for a period of time. Each student would be assigned to teach and/or demonstrate a skill and share some specific knowledge. These skills might include how to mark a trail, build a fire, identify animal tracks, tie knots, read the stars, create tools, construct a shelter, identify edible plants, and deal with the wind and cold (see fig.12).

Excursions

VERBAL

"Aesop's Fables." Younger children might enjoy acting out some of Aesop's fables that deal with hunger and survival. In "The Ant and the Grasshopper," the grasshopper frolics while the ant labors to gather winter provisions. In "The Fox and the Crow," a clever fox uses flattery to steal a meal.

"Jack Frost Plays." Children take turns trying to dissuade Jack Frost from spoiling the harvest. They might try to charm him, flatter him, serenade him, or simply distract him. They should spend some time exploring who Jack Frost is and what his qualities might be, and why frosts can be so damaging to farmers.

"The Birdwatcher and the Hunter." Middle grade and older students might enjoy dramatizing an encounter between a birdwatcher and hunter. The birdwatcher tries all kinds of persuasive arguments to dissuade the hunter from shooting a rare but delicious bird.

"The Factory Debate." Two factory owners who employ many of a town's economically disadvantaged citizens debate two environmentalists who claim the factory is polluting the town's river and air. Should the factory close? Are there any possible compromises that would satisfy both parties?

Survival: Other Ways to Begin	Stories to Tell	Works to Read Aloud	Films to Share
Younger grades Pre-K–2nd	*Arrow to the Sun* (McDermott)	*A Chair for My Mother* (Williams)	*How the Kiwi Lost His Wings*
	"John Henry" (Shapiro)	*Abel's Island* (Steig)	*The Lion and the Mouse*
	Llama and the Great Flood: A Folktale from Peru (Alexander)	*In Coal Country* (Hendershot)	*Dr. De Soto*
	"How the Clever Doctor Cheated Death" (Carter)	*Tuck Everlasting* (Babbitt)	*The Little Fugitive*
Middle grades 3rd–5th	"Molly Whuppie" (Jacobs)	*The Sign of the Beaver* (Speare)	*Where the Lilies Bloom*
	Flame of Peace: A Tale of the Aztecs (Lattimore)	*Boat to Nowhere* (Wartski)	*The Black Stallion*
Upper grades 6th–8th	*The Golem* (Singer)	*Hiroshima No Pika* (Maruki)	*Sugar Cane Alley*
	"The Serpent's Bride" (Berger)	*Somehow Tenderness Survives: Stories of South Africa* (Rochman)	*The Effect of Gamma Rays on Man-in-the-Moon Marigolds*
	The Forever Formula (Bonham)	*Dragonwings* (Yep)	*El Norte*

Fig. 12. Survival: Other Ways to Begin

WRITTEN

"Island Cultures." Student anthropologists write about the lives and ways of imaginary island peoples, describing dwellings, family life, work and play, and important places (homes, paths, forbidden areas, work areas, sacred grounds):

> There was a village on my island, a small secluded one, surrounded by hills, pleasant green hills with a few trees. The people were isolated from all others and there was a little valley with fields enough for just them. The village was in the middle with 12 huts with about eight villagers in each and some cattle outside. The sun would go down and reflect orange in the sky and purple in the clouds. Birds would fly into the sun and turn into black spots. The crops were always plentiful. There was always harmony and laughter, kids playing in the grass by the huts. You would see a parent playing with the kids, or teaching them the necessary skills. It was always joyful as long as they had food. (Cody Campbell, age 11)

> The Emcdom are the high elders of Lak Kackar. They have amazing memories and highly value learning. Learning is passed on in the old way. It is passed on by word of mouth and by example. (Alejo Crawford, age 12)

> There are two villages on our island. The one on the east side of Mulidd River is called Cira, and the village on the west side is called Toona. Both villages get on together very well. They help each other survive. Cira does all the farming, and Toona does all the hunting and gathering. Both villages share the meat, berries, and food from the farm. (Roland Pott, age 12)

Some students enjoy making maps to accompany their writings. These graphic recreations often show some of the more frightening aspects of their imaginary islands (see fig. 13).

"The Junkyard." Objects in a junkyard describe some of the key events in students' lives, joyful and peaceful times, moments of danger. What were their origins? Who were their owners, and how were they treated and used? A broken parasol might describe an outing on the beach. A weather vane might relate its horrific experiences during a storm.

"The Last Tiger." Students imagine what it might be like to be the last living member of a particular species on earth, unable to enjoy the comfort or security of one's own group. Someone could be the last tiger on earth, the last clown, the last flower. The library media specialist may want to read *The Last Free Bird* (Stone).

"The Twilight Zone." The library media specialist shares some of the script summaries from *The Twilight Zone Companion* (Zicree). Many of these deal with the theme of survival. Older children could write television scripts or radio plays in the spirit and style of the series, weaving in ironies, curves, and twists.

Figure 13. Sacred and Forbidden Places on an Imaginary Island (Moses Gardner, age 13). Used with permission

ART AND MUSIC

"Endangered Species Posters." The library media specialist could have children design posters illustrating endangered species. Some students might want to make cutouts, or to sculpt these animals out of clay or play dough.

"Found Object Art." Children create stabiles, collages, or sculptures out of waste materials found around the school and exhibit them to focus on ecological issues and recycling projects.

"Good Luck Mobiles." Children discuss the many kinds of good luck charms that are used as protective devices. They could then make "good luck" mobiles, using drawings and constructions of four-leaf clovers, wishbones, ladybugs, shooting stars, arrowheads, and horseshoes.

"Holocaust Drawings." After sharing with an older group some of the drawings of children in concentration camps from *I Never Saw Another Butterfly*, the library media specialist could have children express, in their own drawings or paintings, the feelings of being cut off from loved ones, of existing behind fences in grey stark realities. What kinds of fantasies would sustain someone in that situation?

"Songs of Protest." Children are introduced to work and protest songs that have helped illuminate the struggles for human and civil rights. They could learn some of the songs of Bob Dylan, Odetta, Pete Seeger, and the Weavers. The library media specialist could share the score of *Sarafina! The Music of Liberation*, which captures the spirit of rebellious South African young people.

RESEARCH

"An Imagination Archive." The library media specialist arranges visits to a museum, library, or film archive so children can find out how works are preserved, and why particular works are chosen for preservation. Some children might learn how to do simple book repairs. Others might be involved in creating a special library archive of students' original stories, poems, and drawings.

"Community Environmental Projects." The library media specialist could have children contact any local environmental groups and find out what issues they are currently involved with, and what strategies they have determined for taking a stand. Is there some way children could assist with particular projects, or link the projects with the school community?

"Oral Histories." Children could interview grandparents and great-grandparents to find out about any of their childhood adventures or scary moments. Did they ever experience a fire, tornado, or earthquake? Did they ever run away? Did they ever get lost or separated from parents? Did they ever have to remain in hiding? Such antecdotes could be turned into a written history.

"A Superstitions Study." Children could first compile a list of superstitions and make posters to illustrate them. They could then examine where superstitions come from and how and why they have survived through time. What superstitions are tied to various cultures? What superstitions have gleamings of truth in them? What are their origins? Why do black cats seem to have such power? Why do the numbers seven and thirteen seem to have extra importance? Some children could create a Superstitions Walk in which others have to crawl under a ladder, knock on a piece of wood, throw salt over their left shoulder, and pet a (stuffed animal) black cat. Some children might want to make up their own humorous superstitions; for example, "Never stare a blind cat in the eye while wearing a monocle." (Chris Egelson, age 11)

"Gypsies." Middle grade and older children research information about gypsies. Where do they come from? How have they survived? Why and how have they been persecuted? What misconceptions exist regarding them? How do they deal with mainstream society? How do children in this culture get educated? Researchers might want to use the book *Gypsies* (Greenfield) as a starting point. Once they collect the information, they could choose to dramatize the gypsy way of life or capture a gypsy celebration through a mural, filmstrip, or slide presentation.

"The Shakers." The library media specialist could have children research information about the Shakers, who they are and how they developed their unique way of life. How will their special arts be preserved? What can new generations learn from them?

"Landmark Buildings." The library media specialist could have children find out the history of various landmark buildings in their communities, and how they qualified for that status. Are there any other buildings that deserve this recognition? How would they build their cases?

Celebrations

"An Archaeological Dig." *When Clay Sings* (Baylor) or *Lost and Found* (Walsh) could be used to stimulate children to think about found objects that could be linked to other cultures and other times. Some children could bring in arrowheads and fossils from home, and other children could try to evaluate their authenticity. A visiting archaeologist, scientist, or museum expert could demonstrate the methods, tools, and instruments used to collect data. The group could then go on an archaeological dig to hunt for artifacts.

"An Old Games Day." An Old Games Day would enable students to learn and experience games that children played years ago, games their grandparents and parents may have grown up with. These games may have been brought here from other cultures and then adapted in some way. Some good print sources to share: *Children's Games in Street and Playground* (Opie); *Shimmy Shimmy Coke-Ca-Pop!* (Langstaff); *Apples on a Stick* (Michels); *Games, Games, Games* (Sandoval). Grandparents and parents could be invited to come as instructors and resource people, and teach such games as stickball, four square, kick the can, and lemonade. At some point, children could be divided into groups and given specific objects (a piece of cloth, two sticks, three pebbles, etc.). They would then be asked to invent a game and teach it to other groups.

"Flying Saucer Day." Children could view Robert Wise's humanistic science fiction film, *The Day the Earth Stood Still*. The storyline involves the arrival on Earth of intelligent beings from another galaxy. They are concerned about this planet's militaristic and destructive ways. The film could be used to provoke discussion on how the Earth will survive in the future. Children, for fun, could be taught the film's protective signature words: "Gort, Klaatu Berrada Nikto." Some children might wish to decorate the walls with posters reflecting their own versions of flying saucers or other worlds from which they have come.

A Journey Log: The "Imaginary Tribes Curriculum"

In the river village, the beast, Antabeakie, is causing considerable harm. It can go on land and water killing both game and fish. Food becomes scarce for the tribe. The bravest warrior sets out to stalk the beast, to follow it for a day, to see how terrible it looks, and to find out its habits and weaknesses. The warrior discovers that the Antabeakie shrivels up at night and becomes very small. She concocts a plan. She gets sap from a magic tree and then looks for two clam shells. She waits that night and covers the sleeping beast with the sticky sap and puts it between the shells and buries it in the earth. The tree becomes sacred because the sap has saved the villagers and it always bears sweet fruit and beautiful blossoms. (Scenario for "The Antabeakie," an eight- and nine-year-old group)

STEP ONE: CHOOSING THE THEME

This curriculum was adapted from my experiences with Richard Lewis and the Touchstone Center for Children in New York City. Doris, the eights/nines teacher, and I were seeking to create a vivid, powerful, and cumulative journey for her students to parallel their study of Eastern Woodland Native Americans. We wanted to thrust them into a situation where they had to operate and achieve harmony in small groups, continually making choices and resolving their differences. We also wanted them to deal with basic survival issues. How could knowledge of the land and its resources be vital?

STEP TWO: PLANNING THE JOURNEY

Doris proved to be a warm, flexible partner who enjoyed the give and take of collaborating. We were able to arrange our schedules to have the whole group together for a ninety-minute session each week. We also met informally every week to evaluate our progress. In the planning stage, we selected some Native American myths, including *Star Boy* (Goble), *Buffalo Woman* (Goble), and *Sedna* (McDermott) to share with each other and then with the children, to prepare them for the journey. We also took a trip to the Museum of Natural History to stimulate our thinking.

STEP THREE: BEGINNING THE JOURNEY

We began our first whole group session with students by examining survival from the point of view of a cactus. "What kind of environment does this plant come from? What are the characteristics of such an environment?" We discussed the possibility of surviving in a desert. "What kinds of dwellings could people build from the materials available? How could they obtain water? How could they make clothing? What animals would people find in this kind of environment?"

STEP FOUR: TAKING SOME EXCURSIONS

The group was then divided into five imaginary tribes: a beach tribe, mountain tribe, lake tribe, river tribe, and flatlands tribe. Each tribe received photographs of their type of terrain, as well as some natural objects. The beach tribe, for example, was given a mussel shell and small piece of driftwood. The first activity involved them in developing a large map that would illustrate and explain some essential places and resources such as dwellings, lookout points, ceremonial grounds, forbidden areas, land and water routes.

The tribes worked three sessions on their maps, collaborating, compromising, working out occasional conflicts. As the maps evolved, stories would naturally begin to grow that explained the origins of things. The maps became very real to them, and children started to identify with their tribes. When asked how they built their shelters or modes of transportation from the natural resources, they seemed challenged and would explain their answers with clarity and pride.

After the maps were finished, the tribes spent one library session creating pantomimes about encounters they might have had coming back to their village after a day's search for food.

In the following session we talked about their mythic or spiritual places. "How did they come into being? What magical events might have happened there? What conflicts may have been resolved? Who emerged as heroes and what were their qualities? What did these places look like? How did a tribe member feel when he or she entered the mythic place?" The children next wrote legends about these sacred places and why they were so important to each tribe.

STEP FIVE: CELEBRATING THE JOURNEY

Students developed the myths into dramatic pieces and presented them to younger classes at the conclusion of the study. They tried to create a strong poetic mood by using a combination of narration, sparse dialog, and pantomime with a rhythmic accompaniment of drums and bells. The myths were interpreted in a dignified and ceremonial manner by their eight- and nine-year-old creators.

There was an astonishing freedom about the way they moved, a thoughtfulness and daring. Teachers commented on how secure they seemed to be as story-tellers, and how much they had identified with the sense of collective power that grew from their tribal studies.

A bully chief lives in the best cave and keeps the best fish for himself. When a giant clam is found on the shore, he makes the people carry the clam up to his chamber. He finds a magic pearl inside of the clam, and soon brags that the pearl grants all his wishes, including jewels, a fine bow, beautiful clothes. A just and courageous boy sneaks into the chamber at night, and hides in the shell. When the evil chief wishes that morning for more riches, the boy in a strange voice tells him to go to the very edge of the cliff, and wait for the seventh flying fish. The chief leans over to spot the fish. He loses his balance, and slips and falls. Naturally, the tribe rejoices. The top of the cliff thereafter becomes the tribe's sacred place. (Scenario for "The Bully Chief and the Giant Clam")

Raiders come to threaten and burn the village unless the people give them every child who will be born in the spring. The raiders say they will return by the next full moon. The villagers seek the advice of the Woman Wizard who lives in the nearby cave. But she is very sick and almost too weak to help them. The Woman Wizard sends the warriors to get dandelion pulp, twigs of gold, and milk from the wild mountain goat so she can regain her magic powers. The warriors go on a long and dangerous quest. They spot the twigs of gold only when the sun's rays first light the earth. The goat is difficult to find, and they must climb to the peak of a thorny ridge. At last they return with the proper ingredients. The Woman Wizard drinks the milk for nourishment and becomes much stronger. She mixes the dandelion pulp with dew and nectar, using the twigs of gold, and she creates a magic paste. She rubs the paste on the hands of all the tribes-people. Then she gives a special feather to the Chief. When the full moon comes, the Chief shakes the feather, and a magical mist prevails. The raiders can't see or find the village. The Woman Wizard's cave, from that time on, becomes the sacred and mythic place of the tribe. (Scenario for "The Woman Wizard and Her Magic")

In a creative-writing session held a week after the play presentations, chil-dren, as members of their tribe, created prayers that descibed their good feelings about the world.

When the sun goes down and the wind starts blowing, you don't know what will happen to you. You start to weep. You can't stop because you have got to give thanks to all the birds and all the air, and the nature that touches your hand. (Lani Nhliziyo, age 9)

REFLECTIONS ON OUTCOMES

Through this exploration, students were introduced to Native American myths and legends. They examined aspects of culture and the roots of cultural anthro-pology. They began to see that all people have the same basic needs as they addressed vital issues concerning survival. They studied the character of geographic regions and became aware of topography and resources. They developed their skills as readers and makers of maps.

Becoming part of a tribe was a visceral experience, and students began to share a tribal identity. As members of a dynamic working group for an extended period, they were enabled to establish common goals, pool talents, and divide the labor fairly. They had to deal with individual differences, to develop techniques for solving problems and resolving conflicts. They were challenged to interpret the worlds they had created from their knowledge of the world of their experience. They explored the supernatural, and created sacred places and ceremonies to honor the mysteries of life. They worked in a variety of media, playing with and expanding their ideas through mapmaking, story making, and creative dramatics. They were able to see their ideas evolve and be expressed in vivid, poetic forms.

References

Books

Alexander, Ellen. *Llama and the Great Flood: A Folktale from Peru*. Crowell, 1989.

Babbitt, Natalie. *Tuck Everlasting*. Farrar, 1975

Baylor, Byrd. *When Clay Sings*, ill. by Tom Bahti. Scribner's, 1972.

Berger, Terry, ed. "The Serpent's Bride" in *Black Fairy Tales*. Atheneum, 1969.

Bonham, Frank. *The Forever Formula*. Dutton, 1979.

Carter, Dorothy Sharp, ed. "How the Clever Doctor Cheated Death" in *Greedy Mariani and Other Folk Tales of the Antilles*. Atheneum, 1974.

Childress, Alice. *A Hero Ain't Nothin' but a Sandwich*. Coward, 1973.

Cleaver, Vera, and Bill Cleaver. *Where the Lilies Bloom*. Lippincott, 1969.

George, Jean. *My Side of the Mountain*. Dutton, 1959.

Goble, Paul. *Buffalo Woman*. Bradbury, 1984.

———. *Star Boy*. Bradbury, 1983.

Greenfield, Howard. *Gypsies*. Crown, 1977.

Hendershot, Judith. *In Coal Country*, ill. by Thomas B. Allen. Knopf, 1987.

Hodges, Margaret. *The Fire Bringer: A Paiute Indian Legend*, ill. by Peter Parnall. Little, 1972.

. . . *I Never Saw Another Butterfly: Children's Drawings and Poems from Terezin Concentration Camp*. McGraw, 1964.

Jacobs, Joseph, ed. "Molly Whuppie" in *English Folk and Fairy Tales*. Putnam. n.d.

Langstaff, John M. *Shimmy Shimmy Coke-Ca-Pop! A Collection of City Children's Games and Rhymes*. Doubleday, 1973.

Lattimore, Deborah Nourse. *The Flame of Peace: A Tale of the Aztecs*. Harper, 1987.

Lionni, Leo. *Swimmy*. Pantheon, 1963.

McDermott, Beverly Brodsky. *Sedna; An Eskimo Myth*. Viking, 1975.

McDermott, Gerald. *Arrow to the Sun; A Pueblo Indian Tale*. Viking, 1974.

Marshall, James Vance. *Walkabout*. Morrow, 1971.

Maruki, Yoshi. *Hiroshima No Pika.* Lothrop, 1980.

Michels, Barbara, and Bettye White, eds. *Apples on a Stick: The Folklore of Black Children.* Coward, 1983.

Opie, Iona. *Children's Games in Street and Playground.* Oxford, 1969.

Pinkwater, Daniel. *Wingman.* Dodd, 1975.

Rochman, Hazel. *Somehow Tenderness Survives: Stories of South Africa.* Harper, 1988.

Sandoval, Ruben. *Games, Games, Games = Juegos, Juegos, Juegos: Chicano Children at Play: Games and Rhymes.* Doubleday, 1977.

Shapiro, Irwin. "John Henry" in *Heros in American Folklore.* Messner, 1962.

Shotwell, Louisa R. *Roosevelt Grady.* World, 1963.

Singer, Isaac Bashevis. *The Golem.* Farrar, 1982.

Speare, Elizabeth. *The Sign of the Beaver.* Houghton, 1983.

Steig, William. *Abel's Island.* Farrar, 1976.

Stone, A. Harris. *The Last Free Bird,* ill. by Sheila Heins. Prentice, 1967.

Uchida, Yoshika. *Journey to Topaz, a Story of the Japanese-American Evacuation.* Scribner's, 1971.

Walsh, Jill Paton. *Lost and Found,* ill. by Mary Rayner. Deutsch, 1984.

Wartski, Maureen Crane. *A Boat to Nowhere.* Westminister, 1980.

Wier, Ester. *The Loner.* McKay, 1963.

Williams, Vera B. *A Chair for My Mother.* Greenwillow, 1982.

Yep, Laurence. *Dragonwings.* Harper, 1975.

Zei, Alki. *Petros' War.* Dutton, 1972.

Zicree, Marc Scott. *The Twilight Zone Companion.* Bantam, 1982.

Films

The Black Stallion, dir. by Carroll Ballard. United Artists, 1979. 125 min.

The Day the Earth Stood Still, dir. by Robert Wise. Fox, 1951. 92 min.

Doctor De Soto. Weston Woods, 1984. 10 min.

The Effect of Gamma Rays on Man-in-the-Moon Marigolds, dir. by Paul Newman. Fox, 1972. 101 min.

El Norte, dir. by Gregory Nava. Island Alive, 1984. 139 min.

How the Kiwi Lost His Wings. Churchill, 1980. 12 min.

The Lion and the Mouse. Benchmark, 1977. 5 min.

The Little Fugitive, dir. by Ray Ashley. Burstyn, 1953. 75 min.

Sugar Cane Alley, dir. by Euzhan Palcy. France, 1984. 103 min.

Where the Lilies Bloom, dir. by William Graham. United Artists, 1974. 97 min.

Recordings and Songs

Sarafina! The Music of Liberation, composed by Mbongeni Ngema. Broadway cast recording. RCA, 1988.

The Fifth Journey:
Bedtime and Nighttime

Introduction to the Study

Bedtime

Bedtime is one of the critical parts of childhood. It represents to children a loss of control, giving up the security and stimulation of others. It is a time when children are less clothed, less protected, and can feel the most vulnerable. When there is no one awake to talk to, children must deal with isolation and confront their anxieties. Naturally, this brings up worries about strange adults and the monsters of the dark. It intensifies the fear of being separated from parents. Whatever a child is storing inside often has a way of surfacing then.

What makes a child feel more at ease when he or she finally goes to bed? A music box? A night light? A teddy bear? Family rituals can help to make bedtime a calming, even joyful, experience. Bedtime can be a time for listening to stories and songs, and for sharing thoughts about the day that has ended or the day that is coming.

Sleep and Dreams

Students could discuss their own sleeping situations, and whether they sleep alone or with others. They could describe their bedrooms—the kinds of beds they have, the kinds of covers and quilts. What's on the wall? Where are the windows? Where is the bathroom? What are the night sounds in their house? What night sounds come from outside the window? What causes sleeping? Why does it seem like such a mysterious process? When are the times people might surrender to sleep, and when are the times they try to fight it? Why do some people sleepwalk, and some people snore? Why do babies sleep so much? Why do older people sometimes rise so early or stay up so late?

The journeys children make at night are mostly through dreams. They can at times vividly recall details, events, sequences, and landscapes. Reconstructing and sharing dreams can help children connect with some of their most powerful feelings and yearnings. In considering dreams, students may want to examine a number of questions. What causes dreams? Do dreams tell stories? Have they ever been lost in a dream? Do they have recurring dreams? What happens to their bodies when they are dreaming? How are dreams perceived and valued in various cultures? Who are the interpreters of dreams?

Have they ever been chased in a dream? Who are the demons, creatures, beasts and scary people who inhabit their nightmares? How would they describe them? Are there ways to protect themselves from bad dreams? How can they make the nightmares go away like the hero in *There's a Nightmare in My Closet* (Mayer)?

Sleeping Away from Home

Sleeping over at a friend's house can raise concerns for children, as depicted in *Ira Sleeps Over* (Waber). What will this other family be like? Will there be a curfew? Will there be snacks? *Pajama Walking* (Artis) shows what a delightful experience sleeping over can be as two friends experiment and make chocolate toothpaste.

Camping out can help children to be resourceful and independent, and to feel comfortable in the woods. There are new kinds of equipment and gear to use: flashlights, compasses, tents, and sleeping bags. There are the possible encounters with raccoons, deer, snakes, and bears. There are the magical surprises of a summer's night sky: swooping owls, satellites, and wishing stars.

Nighttime

What are the sounds of the night? Depending on where they live, children might think of crickets, bells, chimes, whistles, sirens, whispers, murmurs, voices, cries, snores, a blaring radio, a single violin. What are the sounds that make children feel safe? They could then describe sounds that may be hard to identify.

What are the lights of the night? Wherever they live, children may see the moon, stars, plane lights, lampposts, spotlights. Some will know the comfort of lighthouses, ship lights, fireflies, candles, lanterns, campfires. How do these lights assist and comfort people? Have they ever seen a light glow in the dark, but not know the source of it? What stories could they make up about an unknown light?

How do animals sleep? Which ones sleep floating in the sea, and which ones rest in beds of kelp? Which animals prefer a shady cave? A burrow? A hollow tree stump? National Geographic's *Ways Animals Sleep* (McCauley) provides answers to these questions, while *Creatures of the Night* (Rinard) explores the habits and techniques of nocturnal hunters. Joanna Cole's *Large as Life—Night-*

time Animals introduces the more unusual night wanderers: chinchillas, fennec foxes, elf owls, and royal antelopes, no bigger than rabbits.

Who are the night workers? One may think immediately of cab drivers, truckers, bartenders, disc jockeys, doctors, nurses, bakers, and security guards. Who else occupies the night world? How do they keep alert? What adjustments do they have to make in their daily living situations? What do they perceive as the advantages and disadvantages?

How did the earliest people explain the night? What legends and myths have been created about the night sky, about full moons and harvest moons, about comets and constellations? What are some of the Native American myths? Why does looking at the night sky arouse such deep feelings in people, and so often spark their imaginations? In "The Beautiful Girl of the Moon Tower," an American black folktale included in *The People Could Fly* (Hamilton), a young man dreams of a girl who lives on the moon and ponders how he might get there. In *Arrow to the Sun* (McDermott), a Navajo boy must journey to the sky kingdom to discover the secret of his identity.

What are the parts of night? What is the mood at dusk? Why is the night so poetic? What happens when the clock strikes twelve? Why is this sometimes called "the witching hour?" What are the secrets of the night? Uri Shulevitz's *Dawn* captures the magic and stillness of the moments just before sunrise as an old man and his grandson enjoy the privacy of a small lake.

Who are the keepers of the night? Some of them bring comfort and gifts, and provide protection: the tooth fairy, *The Sandman* (Shepperson), *Grandfather Twilight* (Berger), and *The Tomten* (Lindgren). Some of them strike chords of fear in people, and remind them to get home before it is dark: the Headless Horseman, *The Dream Stealer* (Maguire), and the many vampires and werewolves.

Routes

Beginning the Journey

WITH YOUNGER CHILDREN (PRE-K–GRADE 2)

The library media specialist could read aloud *The Napping House* (Wood), in which too many characters share one bed with disastrous and comical results. Children then discuss their own beds and bedrooms. "Did you ever sleep in a bunkbed? A waterbed? A hammock? When you were younger, did you sleep in a crib or a basket? Have you ever fallen out of bed?"

Children could individually design their ideal bedroom, thinking about the kind of bed they would choose, the kinds of furniture and lamps. Someone may even want to create a bedroom that looks like outer space or an undersea world.

After sharing their ideas and designs with each other, they could make models of their ideal bedroom using boxes, carpet scraps, wallpaper samples, cardboard, corks, buttons, and other collage materials.

WITH MIDDLE GRADE CHILDREN (GRADES 3–5)

Children create stories about something magical or poetic that happens on the farm at night. The library media specialist stimulates this by reading aloud *Night in the Country* (Rylant), which captures the gentle sounds and night songs of the country world. Another mood-setting story is *Barn Dance!* (Martin and Archambault), a playful account of animals frolicking in the barn to the tunes of a fiddling scarecrow, and how one skinny kid becomes a part of their secret. After writing their stories, some children might want to act them out or develop them into puppet plays:

At night in the barn, there is a storm. All of the animals are huddled together in the hay. They are very cold but they are sleeping together: chicken, cows, pigs, and sheep, and up above the owl hoots. Suddenly, one of the pigs wakes up and it covers itself with hay and goes back to sleep. And then the owl hoots again and another pig wakes up and covers itself with hay because it is cold. (Cathy Bertchume, age 8)

Once there was a scarecrow that in the day time stood straight and solemn. But strangely the scarecrow did not scare any birds. The farmer got very mad. At night the scarecrow got a lot of birds together and they had a scare-bird party. First a soft-footed sparrow would fly into the barn and get some straw. Then he would take some, throw it up, and use it like confetti. One crow blew up balloons and another crow was singing. The scarecrow was clapping his hands to the rhythm of the music when the first rays of light came. The male birds took off their hats in front of the scarecrow, then put them back on, and flew away while the Sun came up. (Giuliana Chamedes, age 8)

WITH OLDER CHILDREN (GRADES 6-UP)

The library media specialist could play and discuss with children a variety of songs that capture some of the moods of night. "Tonight" from *West Side Story* (Bernstein) sets up a feeling of high expectation. This will be a night of fulfillment and power. "Everybody Loves Saturday Night" speaks universally of the need to release after a hard week at work. "Do You Want to Dance in the Moonlight?" might be interpreted as a lively courtship song. Elton John's "Rocket Man" and the Beatles' "Lucy in the Sky With Diamonds" offer magical imagery and a strong sense of flight.

Older children could then make posters that would illustrate these songs, visually conveying the feelings of the lyrics. They could experiment and do a series of sketches and see which ones are the most effective. They could either work in color or black-and-white (see fig. 14).

Bedtime and Nighttime: Other Ways to Begin	Stories to Tell	Works to Read Aloud	Films to Share
Younger grades Pre-K–2nd	"How Fisher Went to the Skyland: The Origin of the Big Dipper" (Caduto)	*When I'm Sleepy* (Howard)	*Lullaby*
	The Nightingale (Andersen)	*Polar Express* (Van Allsburg)	*Moonbird*
	Why the Sun and Moon Live in the Sky: An African Folktale (Dayrell)	*Owl Moon* (Yolen)	*A Night in a Pet Shop*
Middle grades 3rd–5th	*The Iron Giant: A Story in Five Nights* (Hughes)	*The Moon's Revenge* (Aiken)	*The Fur Coat Club*
	"Rairu and the Star Maiden" (Finger)	*The Night Swimmers* (Byars)	*The Magic Bow*
	The Firebird (Kemp)	*The House of Dies Drear* (Hamilton)	*Cornet at Night*
Upper grades 6th–8th	"The Man Who Came Out at Night" (Calvino)	*The Halloween Tree* (Bradbury)	*Stand by Me*
	"The Fire on the Mountain" (Courlauder)	*The Night Journey* (Lasky)	*The Night of the Hunter*
	"The Power of Light" (Singer)	*Night Cry* (Naylor)	*A Night at the Opera*

Fig. 14. Bedtime and Nighttime: Other Ways to Begin

Excursions

VERBAL

"Sound Worlds." Younger children use a tape recorder to create simulated sound environments of various night worlds: a desert, park, seashore, zoo, circus. What are the individual sounds? How do the sounds change when there is a storm? What might happen when a stranger enters these worlds?

"Shoebox Theaters." Pairs of children create Popsicle-stick puppets and shoebox theaters, and then devise plays about spending the night in a famous building (museum, aquarium, concert hall, gallery, opera house, planetarium, sculpture garden, tower). What magical or mysterious things could happen there? They might at first want to describe and discuss the adventures that took place in *From the Mixed-Up Files of Mrs. Basil E. Frankweiler* (Konigsburg), when two runaways spend the night at New York's Metropolitan Museum.

"Keepers of the Night." Middle grade and older children create their own plays about the keepers of the night. Who are these keepers? How do they speak and move? What do they wear? What happens on their journeys? How do they help or harm others? How did they come to be? What are their stories? A terrific sourcebook for this project would be *The Book of the Sandman and the Alphabet of Sleep* (Poortvliet).

WRITTEN

"Dream Books." Younger children, after being encouraged to share some of their dreams, create dream books in which they describe and illustrate three of their own dreams: one that is beautiful, one that is funny, and one that is scary.

> This is me dreaming of a pig. My feet were buried in slop. I was spraying slop in the air. It was fun. I ate the farmer's leftovers. (Eric Thorsen, age 8)

> This is what I want to dream about. It's a special place. It has a green door, and purple steps, and a diving board. You dive into a warm pool. You eat apples if you are hungry. You can walk on the rainbow. (Kunio Hori, age 8)

"The Witching Hour." Sophie, the heroine in *The BFG* (Dahl), anticipates the witching hour when "all the dark things came out from hiding and had the world to themselves." Children could describe the "witching hour" in their own words, based on their experiences or fantasies:

> You can hear ghosts laughing loud. They are planning to get someone. The witches are making a spell. (Amelia Krales, age 8)

> When all the evil things come out. It's just before the sun comes up and everything is still. Nothing moves. (Britt Morgan-Saks, age 8)

When everyone falls into a trance—when the sandman comes, and you hear sand scratching. (Adam Ellenhorn, age 8)

"Lights of the Night." *The Little Red Lighthouse and the Great Gray Bridge* (Swift and Ward) suggests how a light in the darkness can provide comfort and lead people to safety. This work can be used effectively to stimulate storywriting about other lights of the night.

A knight lived in a castle on the moon. He shot an arrow to the earth. The arrow whizzed by some people camping by a fire, and picked up a medium kid, and took him up to the castle. The knight was alone and needed a friend. The kid was happy because he always wanted to go to the sky. (Lucas Nivon, age 7)

Once a little boy was sleeping. He was six years old, and he didn't know how to spell. He was dreaming of a cobra snake when a little roach came and crawled up his leg. Then a light came through the hole in the roof of his tent. It shined on the roach, and it was so bright that the roach couldn't stand it. The roach died and a greedy cricket ate it for a snack. Then the light kissed the boy on the cheek. (Halsey Chait, age 7)

ART AND MUSIC

"Stages of Night Mural." Children create a mural depicting the stages of night: twilight, darkest night, the time before daybreak. They might describe first the things one might see and hear at each particular stage. What might be some of the obvious changes that may take place in a specific environment during the course of one night? What might be some of the subtle changes?

"Nightmare Factory." Children bring to life a nightmare factory. Using brown paper, cardboard, and drawing or painting materials, small groups of children would be responsible for creating particular parts of the nightmare's body (ears, head, neck, arms, hands, trunk, legs, feet). Finally, the nightmare could be put together and given a name. He or she could become the library mascot. Some children might want to make up poems, stories, or legends about their nightmare, or even create plays or films.

"Lullabies." How do lullabies nourish children preparing for sleep? The library media specialist could read aloud some lullabies from *Lullabies and Night Songs* (Engvick) and *Dragon Nights and Other Lullabies* (Yolen) and then have children compose their own lullabies and night songs.

RESEARCH

"Plants and Animals at Night." Children investigate what happens to plants, insects, amphibians, and reptiles at night. They could do actual observations at home or on campouts. They then develop an exhibit to share some of their outcomes.

"The Longest Night." Children ask individuals of all ages to describe the "longest night" of their lives. Did this night involve waiting for a birth, getting lost, studying for an exam, waiting up with someone who was sick? They could then develop some of their materials into dramatic pieces.

"Night Workers." Students locate information about night workers and their occupations. Why is it necessary to work at night? Are there any special advantages? Students could interview some of the people who work at night, and find out how this affects personal relationships, and leisure time activities. Perhaps they could invite three or four night workers to come to their school and present their perceptions as members of a panel.

"Sleeping and Dreaming." Younger children might investigate sleep, why it is necessary, and what happens to their bodies when they are sleep. Older students might study various approaches to dream analysis: how psychologists interpret dreams, how the Australian Aborigines describe the "waking self" and the "dreaming self," and how the Plains Native Americans experience their "sacred dream world."

Celebrations

"A Bat Festival." What does it mean to be batty, or to have "bats in one's belfry"? Children could explore why people are so fascinated with bats. What myths and misconceptions have evolved regarding them? Why and how have these gotten started? What are the true characteristics of these much-maligned nocturnal mammals? During the "Bat Festival," children would conduct lively seminars to promote a better understanding of these creatures. They might also want to present a slide show, read aloud original poems or passages from *The Bat-Poet* (Jarrell), and pass out hand-printed "Bat Awareness" buttons.

"Trip to the Planetarium." A celebration of the night sky culminates in a visit to the planetarium. Beforehand, children could learn and share some Native American legends about the stars and moon. Two excellent sourcebooks are *Star Tales* (Mayo) and *They Dance in the Sky: Native American Star Myths* (Monroe). An afternoon follow-up activity might involve children in making simple telescopes or even their own miniature planetariums.

"The Magic Practitioners' First Annual Nocturnal Convention." This would be a coming together of elves, fairies, leprechauns, trolls, wizards, warlocks, and witches. At this late-night costumed gathering, they could exchange recipes and spells, buy and sell products, and conduct and attend workshops examining the problems and pitfalls they encounter in their work. A magic show could, naturally, highlight the festivities.

"A Sleepy Hollow Festival." This celebration would recreate the flavor and texture of the Catskills in honor of Washington Irving. Children listen to authentic Catskills music, and engage in square dancing and a Brom Bones storytelling contest. Those who wanted could draw or paint their impressions of the Headless Horseman. Some children might dramatize scenes from *The Legend of*

Sleepy Hollow (Irving), perhaps one of Ichabod Crane conducting a class, or the scene where he meets and falls in love with Katrina Van Tassel.

A Journey Log: The "Night Curriculum"

My dream place is a zoo. I sometimes take rides. I go to the cages and feed the antelope. Once I fed a sheep. He didn't say anything, but he made pattering with his feet. (Carla Aspenberg, age 7)

STEP ONE: CHOOSING THE THEME

All children are deeply concerned about nighttime, but their feelings and perceptions may rarely be examined in the classroom. In the library program, extended, open-ended discussions can encourage children to talk freely about both their dreams and their worries about the dark.

I had always hoped to tap into this theme at some point and explore its content with students in some depth. I wanted to provide them with an experience in which they could express all their feelings about the night and begin to appreciate the rich universal heritage of night lore, lullabies, poems, stories, and myths.

STEP TWO: PLANNING THE JOURNEY

Our music teacher, Susan, was also excited about this theme, and we were able to work together as partners to create a curriculum. We decided to explore the theme with the four youngest groups, ages four through eight years, over a period of eight weeks. Although we emphasized the more comforting, poetic aspects of night, we also wanted children to examine their anxieties and fantasies about night and darkness. We brainstormed for several sessions, listing a number of possible routes to take with the theme. Finally, we presented our ideas in a meeting with lower school teachers. They immediately picked up on the theme and expanded our thinking with their suggestions for projects and materials. Helen, the science teacher, volunteered to develop a special ongoing "night" display in the library.

STEP THREE: BEGINNING THE JOURNEY

I began the journey with all four age groups by telling and reading aloud stories about the night world, stories with strong emotional currents that would provoke exciting discussions. *Hildilid's Night* (Ryan) presents a feisty old woman who is determined to chase the night away. Children enjoyed adding to her list of things she hated about the night. *The Angry Moon* (Sleator) retells a Native American legend about a girl who is captured by the moon and held prisoner. The story aroused children to describe some of their fears, especially fears about being separated from parents. *The Ghost-Eye Tree* (Martin and Archambault) also triggered strong discussions about night fears. In this darkly poetic book, a country boy is obsessed with a tree he must pass on his journeys into town.

STEP FOUR: TAKING SOME EXCURSIONS

In the music program, children improvised the movement of stars and shooting stars, and of different animals sleeping and waking. They learned a variety of night songs, including spirituals, rounds, and lullabies.

In the library program, children learned what caused them to sleep, and what in nature creates light and darkness. The fours/fives listened to stories about night flights, and legends about the moon and stars. The fives/sixes designed and built miniature bedrooms. The sevens/eights made sound tapes of night environments. The sixes/sevens described their dreams and created dream books (see fig. 15).

STEP FIVE: CELEBRATING THE JOURNEY

To celebrate our exploration of the night world, Susan and I envisioned a night festival where all four groups could come together and share their songs, stories, and perceptions of the night. We met individually with the four head teachers and with a small group of sixth grade library assistants who had volunteered to help us. We finally decided on having a wedding between Day and Night. Such an activity, we thought, would provide us with a structure, a ceremony, and a sense of festivity. Each of the four groups would bring handmade wedding gifts for the bride and groom and make a musical or dramatic presentation of some aspect or dimension of night. The children would work on these projects for the next three weeks during music, library, and special class times.

The youngest group of four- and five-year-olds adapted "The Seven Jumps," a lively Danish circle dance that begins with skipping around and putting elbows on the floor. They made simple moon costumes and moon hats, using yellow construction and crepe paper. They also created little clothespin moon puppets with big moon heads to give as wedding gifts.

The five- and six-year-olds worked on a performance of "The Fox Went Out on a Chilly Night," a song about a fox who goes out to steal chickens from a farmer so he can feed his hungry wife and children. The farmer and his wife wore nightcaps, and the foxes and their many children wore ears and tails. The fives/sixes made telescopes as their wedding gifts, using cardboard tubes and colored cellophane paper.

The six- and seven-year-olds collaboratively developed stories in half groups about the imaginary sky people and how they lived and worked. They acted out these stories, using narration and mime. Their gifts included homemade cardboard appliances and furniture (a lamp, toaster oven, rocking chair).

The seven- and eight-year-olds worked with Susan to create a vocal and instrumental version of the folk song, "The Lion Sleeps Tonight." The song had

Fig. 15. A Scary Dream (Rother Schlager, age 7). Used with permission

Once I dreamed I went
to climb a big mountain
and meet a wolf and
see the big big sun.
That was my dream.
The End.

Fig. 15—*Continued*

a hushed, lilting quality as they practiced with bells, drums, tambourines, and rhythm sticks. This group wrote poems about the night to give as gifts to the bride and groom.

The sixth grade assistants supervised small groups of children in creating a mural of the night sky that exploded with rockets, comets, and shooting stars. They created Day and Night bride and groom puppets that were two feet tall, and helped me plan and compose the wedding ceremony.

Finally, the wedding arrived. Susan played a welcoming song on the piano as the youngest groups gathered in the music room. The room looked handsome; the night sky mural decorating the main wall served as a backdrop for all the performances. To begin, everyone joined in the singing of the round, "Oh, How Lovely Is the Evening." Its sweetness and simplicity set the tone for the celebration. Then I narrated the story of the Sky People as small groups of six- and seven-year-olds pantomimed the words with only a minimum of props:

> The Sky People are puffy looking. They wear cloud clothes. They are so magical that they can get close to the Sun without burning. They live in houses right next to the sky fields. The Sky People like to play in the air. They dance. They flip. They jump over the loop. They play with pots and pans, banging and making strange noises. The Sky People write with capital letters and talk with vowels. They can speak four languages: snow language, rain language, hail language, and fog language.

The Sky People dust the clouds and keep the sky clean. They put a special kind of wax on the moon to make it shine, and they rub hard. In the Sky Forest, the trees are ten feet tall. The old knight guards the forest. He guards everything that is important: the white berries, the yellow-brown squirrels. Every two years the magic moon ray beams down and makes a new child, and the sky people dance and celebrate.

The four- and five-year-olds performed "The Dance of the Seven Moons," skipping and moving around spiritedly even as most of their moon hats fell onto the floor.

The seven- and eight-year-olds presented "The Lion Sleeps Tonight." Their voices were strong and the effect of the drums was quite haunting.

"John! John! The grey goose is gone!" sang out the frantic farmer's wife as the five- and six-year-olds acted out "The Fox Went Out on a Chilly Night." The bewildered farmer then half sung and half spoke his lines in the tradition of Rex Harrison.

At last I announced the marriage ceremony. The lights were dimmed as live sweet music began to play. There was a definite mood of solemnity, a quiet exuberance. The Day puppet appeared from behind the podium. She had a smiling sun face. The Night puppet then joined her. His face was an elegant half moon. One of the sixth graders, Oak, dressed in a blue suit and black silk hat, acted as the justice of the peace.

"People of the Universe," he began. "We have come together today to witness the wedding of eternity—the wedding between Day and Night. What do you say, Day and Night? What do you promise to the people everywhere?"

"I, Day," spoke the Sun puppet, "will give you each warmth so you can grow things and be active and healthy. I will give you brightness, so you can find things, and take a stroll with your friends." "I, Night," spoke the Moon puppet, "will shade you and cool you so you can sleep and get the rest that you need. I will give you light for journeys in the dark, light from my moon and stars so you won't feel so scared."

The justice of the peace cleared his throat. "You have spoken from the heart, and, from now on, you will be joined in harmony."

The children beamed and applauded as Susan played "Here Comes the Bride." A few children from each group came up to present their wedding gifts: the moon puppets, the cardboard furniture, the telescopes and night poems.

I announced that, in honor of the marriage, a special visitor had traveled all the way from the evening sky to perform for Day and Night and the people of the school. A hush fell over the music room. A calliope tune played gently.

"Here is the one person who can spin and turn gracefully in and out of the craters of the moon. Here is the moonrider."

A sixth grader, dressed simply in black, came riding out on his unicycle. He circled around at different speeds, almost gliding at times, moving a breath away from the children. The effect was dazzling. After the moonrider bicycled away, we all joined in the singing of the spiritual, "My Lord, What a Mornin'." It really had seemed that we had celebrated through the night, and that something important had happened.

REFLECTIONS ON OUTCOMES

"Night" proved to be the perfect theme for the wondering child. It helped children to see that dreams were important, and the sharing of bad dreams may have helped to ease some of their fears. It linked them universally to all children and grown-ups, as sleepers and dreamers, and as individuals who must separate each night, and deal with their aloneness. It allowed them to consider those cosmic and spiritual questions. Why do the moon and stars so deeply arouse and inspire us? How did they get there? How does science explain them? And what do the poets say?

Throughout the exploration, children were introduced to a variety of works, including lullabies and songs, folk dances, information books, picture storybooks, and Native American myths and legends. They were able to experiment with materials, and work in many art forms, often combining them as in the sixes/sevens group's "Sky People" project, which involved collaborative storymaking, with children first dictating and writing their ideas, then pooling them and, finally, dramatizing a cohesive, fluid work. The project also utilized their music skills in the creating of chants, and their art skills in the making of simple props. The entire process was organic and rooted in their imaginations.

The wedding ceremony allowed us to come together in a way that was thoughtful and different, and to share in the unfolding of a magical story. There was the true feeling of giving and sharing, and a clear sense of belonging. We had now become an aesthetic community, a poetic community, and everyone accepted the element of "make believe." Children knew this was not a real wedding, but it became real to them in a symbolic sense. All the proceedings had a freshness, since there had been no full rehearsals. From time to time there would be a lull, a quiet, a kind of collective hush. What was going to happen next? And as one of the two in charge, I would hold my breath, and wonder a little myself.

References

Books

Aiken, Joan. *The Moon's Revenge,* ill. by Alan Lee. Knopf, 1987.
Andersen, Hans Christian. *The Nightingale,* ill. by Demi. Harcourt, 1985.
Artis, Vicki K. *Pajama Walking,* ill. by Emily Arnold McCully. Houghton, 1981.
Berger, Barbara. *Grandfather Twilight.* Philomel, 1984.

Bradbury, Ray. *The Halloween Tree*. Knopf, 1972.

Byars, Betsy. *The Night Swimmers*. Delacorte, 1980.

Caduto, Michael, and Joseph Bruchac. "How Fisher Went to the Skyland: The Origin of the Big Dipper" in *Keepers of the Earth: Native American Stories and Environmental Activities for Children*. Fulcrum, 1988.

Calvino, Italo. "The Man Who Came Out at Night" in *Italian Folktales*. Harcourt, 1980.

Cole, Joanna. *Large as Life—Nighttime Animals*, ill. by Kenneth Lilly. Knopf, 1985.

Courlander, Harold, and Wolf Leslau. "The Fire on the Mountain" in *The Fire on the Mountain and Other Ethiopian Stories*. Holt, 1950.

Dahl, Roald. *The BFG*. Farrar, 1982.

Dayrell, Elphinstone, *Why the Sun and Moon Live in the Sky: An African Folktale*, ill. by Blair Lent. Houghton, 1968.

Engvick, William, ed. *Lullabies and Night Songs*, ill. by Maurice Sendak. Harper, 1965.

Finger, Charles J. "Rairu and the Star Maiden" in *Tales from Silver Lands*. Doubleday, 1924.

Hamilton, Virginia. *The House of Dies Drear*. Macmillan, 1968.

———. "The Beautiful Girl of the Moon Tower" in *The People Could Fly: American Black Folktales*, ill. by Leo and Diane Dillon. Knopf, 1985.

Howard, Jane R. *When I'm Sleepy*, ill. by Lynne Cherry. Dutton, 1985.

Hughes, Ted. *The Iron Giant: A Story in Five Nights*, ill. by Robert Nadler. Harper, 1988.

Irving, Washington. *The Legend of Sleepy Hollow*, retold by Robert D. San Souci and ill. by Daniel San Souci. Doubleday, 1986.

Jarrell, Randall. *The Bat-Poet*, ill. by Maurice Sendak. Macmillan, 1963.

Kemp, Moira. *The Firebird*. Godine, 1984.

Konigsburg, Elaine. *From the Mixed-Up Files of Mrs. Basil E. Frankweiler*. Atheneum, 1967.

Lasky, Kathryn. *The Night Journey*. Warne, 1982.

Lindgren, Astrid. *The Tomten*, ill. by Harald Wiberg. Coward 1961.

McCauley, Jane R. *Ways Animals Sleep*. National Geographic, 1983.

McDermott, Gerald. *Arrow to the Sun: A Pueblo Indian Tale*. Viking, 1974.

Maguire, Gregory. *The Dream Stealer*. Harper, 1983.

Martin Jr., Bill, and John Archambault. *Barn Dance!* ill. by Ted Rand. Holt, 1986.

———. *The Ghost-Eye Tree*, ill. by Ted Rand. Holt, 1985.

Mayer, Mercer. *There's a Nightmare in My Closet*. Dial, 1968.

Mayo, Gretchen. *Star Tales: North American Indian Stories about the Stars*. Walker, 1987.

Monroe, Jean Guard. *They Dance in the Sky: Native American Star Myths*. Houghton, 1987.

Naylor, Phyllis Reynolds. *Night Cry*. Atheneum, 1984.

Poortvliet, Rien. *The Book of the Sandman and the Alphabet of Sleep*, text by Wil ·Huygen. Abrams, 1989.

Rinard, Judith E. *Creatures of the Night*. National Geographic, 1977.

Ryan, Cheli D. *Hildilid's Night*, ill. by Arnold Lobel. Macmillan, 1971.

Rylant, Cynthia. *Night in the Country*, ill. by Mary Szilagy. Bradbury, 1986.

Shepperson, Rob. *The Sandman*. Farrar, 1990.

Shulevitz, Uri. *Dawn*. Farrar, 1974.

Singer, Isaac Bashevis. "The Power of Light" in *The Power of Light: Eight Stories for Hannukah*. Farrar, 1980.

Sleator, William. *The Angry Moon*, ill. by Blair Lent. Little, 1970.

Swift, Hildegarde H., and Lynd Ward. *The Little Red Lighthouse and the Great Gray Bridge*. Harcourt, 1942.

Van Allsburg, Chris. *Polar Express*. Houghton. 1985.

Waber, Bernard. *Ira Sleeps Over*. Houghton. 1972.

Wood, Audrey. *The Napping House*, ill. by Don Wood. Harcourt, 1984.

Yolen, Jane. *Dragon Nights and Other Lullabies*, ill. by Demi. Methuen, 1980.

———. *Owl Man*, ill. by John Schoenherr. Philomel, 1987.

Films

Cornet at Night. Atlantis, 1984. 25 min.

The Fur Coat Club. Learning Corporation, 1973. 18 min.

Lullaby. International Film Bureau, 1977. 3:30 min.

The Magic Bow. McGraw-Hill, 1968. 13 min.

Moonbird. McGraw-Hill, 1959. 10 min.

A Night at the Opera, dir. by Sam Wood. MGM, 1935. 90 min.

A Night in a Pet Shop. McGraw-Hill, 1950s. 14 min.

The Night of the Hunter, dir. by Charles Laughton. United Artists, 1955. 93 min.

Stand by Me, dir. by Rob Reiner. Columbia, 1986. 87 min.

Recordings and Songs

"Do You Wanna Dance?" in *The Divine Miss M*, composed by Bobby Freeman and sung by Bette Midler. Atlantic, 1972.

"Everybody Loves Saturday Night" in *The New Christie Minstrels' Greatest Hits (audio recording)*. Columbia, 1966.

"The Fox Went Out on a Chilly Night" in *Go In and Out the Window: An Illustrated Song Book for Young People*. Holt, 1987.

"The Lion Sleeps Tonight" (listed as "Wimoweh") in *The Weavers Reunion at Carnegie Hall 1963 (audio recording)*. Vanguard, 1987.

"Lucy in the Sky with Diamonds" in *Sgt. Pepper's Lonely Hearts Club Band* (audio recording). Words and music by John Lennon and Paul McCartney. Capitol, 1967.

"My Lord, What a Mornin' " in *The Books of American Negro Spirituals*, ed. by James Weldon Johnson (book). Da Capo Press, 1969.

"Oh, How Lovely Is the Evening," a traditional round in *Music and You* (book). Macmillan, 1988.

"Rocket Man" in *Elton John's Greatest Hits* (audio recording). MCA, 1974.

"The Seven Jumps," a Danish folkdance in *Folk Dances Near and Far*. RCA, 1980.

"Tonight" in *West Side Story*. Words and music by Stephen Sondheim and Leonard Bernstein. Original soundtrack. Columbia, 1961.

While working as a professional school librarian, Gary Zingher has also been active in writing and creative dramatics. He received his MLS from St. John's University where he was the 1980 recipient of the H. W. Wilson Scholarship. Zingher is the co-developer and co-teacher of the Creative Library Programs course at the Bank Street College of Education in New York City.

The paper used in this publication meets the minimum requirements of American National Standard for Information Sciences—Permanence of Paper for Printed Library Materials, ANSI Z39.48-1984. ∞

Cover illustration by Marcus Arrington,
  Manhattan Country School
Text designed by Peter Broeksmit

Composed by Alexander Typesetting, Inc., in
  Times Roman on a Datalogics composition
  system and output on a Linotronic 202

Printed on 50-pound Glatfelter, a pH-neutral
  stock, and bound in 10-point Carolina cover
  stock by Edwards Brothers, Inc.